BINKY'S GUIDE TO

Love

KU-260-197

A CARTOON BOOK BY MATT GROENING

OTHER "HELL" BOOKS BY YOUR CARTOON PAL

LOVE IS HELL

WORK IS HELL

SCHOOL IS HELL

CHILDHOOD IS HELL

AKBAR & JEFF'S GUIDE TO LIFE

THE BIG BOOK OF HELL

HOW TO GO TO HELL

THE ROAD TO HELL

WORKS IN PROGRESS

BINKY'S GUIDE TO HATE

BINKY'S GUIDE TO AMBIVALENCE

BINKY'S GUIDE TO BICKERING

BINKY'S GUIDE TO SCREECHING AND YELLING

BINKY'S GUIDE TO THE SILENT TREATMENT

BINKY'S GUIDE TO APOLOGIZING

Binky's Guide to Love. Copyright © 1994 by Matt Groening Productions, Inc. All rights reserved. Printed in Mexico. No part of this book may be used or reproduced in any manner whatsoever without written permission except in the case of brief quotations embodied in critical articles and reviews. For information address HarperCollins Publishers, Inc., 10 East 53rd Street, New York, NY 10022.

The cartoons in this work were originally published as part of the Life in Hell ® cartoon newspaper syndication, Copyright © 1989, 1990, 1991, 1992, 1993, 1994 by Matt Groening.

HarperCollins books may be purchased for educational, business, or sales promotional use. For information, please write: Special Markets Department, HarperCollins Publishers, Inc., 10 East 53rd Street, New York, NY 10022.

First Edition

COVER AND INTERIOR DESIGN: Cindy Vance

INDEXING, STUDY QUESTIONS, AND OTHER CREATIVE JUICES: Jamie Angell

EDITOR: Wendy Wolf

LEGAL COUNSEL: Susan Grode

ETERNAL THANKS TO: Sondra Gatewood, Jeannine Crowell, Annette Andersen, Eileen Campion, Julie Steddom Smith, and the radiant Deborah Caplan

LYNDA BARRY IST DIE FUNK-QUEEN WESTLICH DER ROCKIES

ISBN 0-06-095078-1

94 95 96 97 98 RRD 10 9 8 7 6 5 4 3 2 1

TABLE OF CONTENTS

Chapter I: What's Your Problem? 7

Chapter II: The Curse of Love 8

Chapter III: The Dart Game of Love, or "Pin the Tail on Your Inner Donkey" 9

Chapter IV: Love Psychoanalyzed, Without Once Using the Word "Codependent" 10

Chapter V: What Does Love Feel Like? 11

Chapter VI: The Weird World of Ambivalence 12

Chapter VII: Is the Water-Glass of Love Half-Empty or Half-Full? 13

Chapter VIII: The Shameful Hidden Taboo Roots of Your Search for Love 14

Chapter IX: The Joys of Lovelessness 15

Chapter X: Fear of Rejection 16

Chapter XI: Why You're So Screwed Up: The Briefest of Overviews 17

Chapter XII: 9 Common Ruts 18

Chapter XIII: Are You Doomed? 19

Chapter XIV: 16 Signs That You're Ready for Love 20

Chapter XV: Questions for the Single Man 21

Chapter XVI: Questions for the Single Woman 22

Chapter XVII: Questions for the Love Experts 23

Chapter XVIII: You Must Sell Yourself for Love 24

Chapter XIX: Dare a Woman Make the First Move? 25

Chapter XX: Questionable Opening Lines 26

Chapter XXI: More Questionable Opening Lines 27

Chapter XXII: The Mating Dance for Beginners 28

Chapter XXIII: The Magical Foolishness of Love 29

Chapter XXIV: 6 Tormenting Love Questions 30

Chapter XXV: First-Date Conversational No-Nos 31

Chapter XXVI: What to Think About on the First Date 32

Chapter XXVII: Will Staring at the Phone Long Enough Make Him Call You?: A Scientific Experiment 33

How Would You Describe Our Relationship? 34

Of Course I'm Guilty 35

We're Stuck in a Rut 36

You're Not Doing It Right 37

Akbar 'n' Jeff's Beachside Souvenir 'n' Snack Hut 38

Are You Ready to Embrace Family Values Yet? 39

Secrets of the Creative 40

Explain Family Values 41

Talk Dirty to Me 42

Maybe the Republicans Are Right 43

Getting Your Head Chopped Off By a Guillotine Would Be Weird 44

Binky's Guide to Our Musical Roots 45

What Were We Thinking? 46

Love? Hate! 47

And You'll Stay in There Until You Learn Some Proper Respect for Authority 48

Are You Trying to Break Up with Me? 49

Kids Want to Know 50

Whenever I Raise a Difficult Subject, Your Response Is to Leave the Room 51

We're Just a Couple of Frisky Little Bounce-Bunnies 52

How to Keep From Exploding with Rage 53

The Return of the Dinosaur Pop-Up Book 54

Let's Fight to the Death 55

Akbar & Jeff's Support Group for the Vaguely Dissatisfied 56

Merry Xmas Anyway 57

No! We Mustn't! 58

How to Cheer Up a Disgruntled New Mother: A Sad But True Story 59

Do You Love Me? 60

You've Got to Stop This Destructive Cycle of Hurtful Conflict 61

The Joy of Cartoon Fame 62

I Missed You 63

Coffee Break's Over, Binky 64

If You Don't Tell Me You Love Me, I Think My Head Is
Going to Explode 65

If You Think I'm Going to Respond to Your Head Exploding 66

At Least We're Not Fighting Anymore.....................67

Akbar & Jeff's Official L.A. Riots Souvenir T-Shirts 68

The More You Talk About People Starving in Somalia 69

How to Stop a Throbbing Headache 70

Akbar & Jeff's Tattoo Hut 71

You're Naked 72

Have We Lost Our Minds?......................................73

You've Never Explained Why the Cartoon Is Called "Life in Hell" 74

How to Get Beyond Stress 75

Important Questions About Monsters 76

Bedtime Story, by Will Groening and His Dad 77

Are You Sure This Is Safe?....................................78

Akbar & Jeff's Piercing Hut 79

The Ballad of Akbar & Jeff 80

The Legend of God, by Will, with Commentary by Abe 81

Your Flu Checklist 82

Daddy! You're the Daddy Lion 83

Life in Hell 10th Anniversary Strip: Quiet, Please 84

Binky's Search for Enlightenment 85

Hexxon 86

I'm Sorry About Last Night 87

Tell Me Another Story, Daddy 88

I Think This Has Been Our Best Group Session Yet 89

My Therapist Says 90

Daddy! I Got a Haircut 91

The Sad Part Is They Think They're Happy 92

A Brief History of My Lousy Mood 93

Are You Trying to Break Up with Me?....................94

So How Was School Today? 95

Akbar & Jeff's "Sex" 96

In a Sense, We Are Both Winners 97

We're Bombing Iraq Again 98

I Think I've Captured Your Good Side....................99

What Will You Do If I Die Before You? 100

Akbar & Jeff's Library..101

Why Is the TV Saying America Is Proud Again?....................102

Skoodly-Oodly-Doodly-Doo 103

I Hope You Kids Learn the Lesson "3 Strikes You're Out" 104

I Could Stab You and Kill You................................105

Y'Know, Bongo, I Had a Lotta Problems with My Dad When
I Was Growing Up 106

I Pledge Allegiance to Frank Zappa........................107

I Put Some Prozac In Your Cornflakes This Morning.....................108

Akbar & Jeff's Couples Therapy Center....................109

Why Did the U.S. Government Conduct Secret Radiation
Tests on Unsuspecting Teenaged Boys? 110

A Brief History of Anger 111

As Long As We Realize How Unhappy We Really Are, We Can Be
Together Forever..112

Remember Now . . . Do Not Open Till Christmas! 113

Am I Going to Die, Daddy?......................................114

Do You Love Me?..115

I'll Give You 30 Seconds to Say I Love You or I'm Leaving
You Forever 116

You Lied to Me..117

Yikes! For a Second There I Had a Fleeting Sensation of
Spiritual Emptiness! 118

Extra Sprinkles, Please 119

I Just Realized Something..120

We Better Take Our Prozac 121

I Love Happy Endings..122

STUDY QUESTIONS..123

INDEX..125

LIFE IN HELL

© 1992 BY MATT GROENING KAUAI

BINKY'S GUIDE TO LOVE
ADVICE FOR THE CONFUSED BY AN EXPERT

I'M BINKY. I'LL BE YOUR WAITER. I MEAN, YOUR LOVE GUIDE.

CHAPTER I:
WHAT'S YOUR PROBLEM?

LOVE SECRET #1
DIFFERENT PEOPLE MEAN DIFFERENT THINGS AT DIFFERENT TIMES WHEN THEY USE THE WORD "LOVE." BEWARE.

DO YOU LOVE ME?

I LOVE YOU AS MUCH AS I LOVE THIS BOWL OF CHILI.

AND I L-O-O-O-V-E CHILI.

COME ON, ADMIT IT.
YOU HAVE A PROBLEM.

WELL, I'M NOT SURE IF I REALLY, LIKE, HAVE A PROBLEM.

OH, COME OFF IT. LOOK AROUND YOU. WHAT DO YOU SEE? HAPPY, SMILING, NUZZLING, GROPING COUPLES FEEDING EACH OTHER GRAPES, GIGGLING IN THE RAIN, TALKING BABY TALK, GAZING INTO EACH OTHER'S EYES, RAMMING EACH OTHER JOYFULLY IN BUMPER CARS, GRABBING EACH OTHER'S THIGHS UNDER THE CAFE TABLE WHEN THEY THINK NO ONE IS LOOKING...

AND THERE YOU SIT, ALONE WITH YOUR ACHING NECK AND YOUR CUP OF COLD, BITTER COFFEE--BITTER LIKE YOUR SOUL, FULL OF RANCID, CHURNED-UP GROUNDS EATING AWAY AT YOUR HATEFUL LITTLE LIFE. MAYBE YOU SHOULD GET A GUN AND KILL YOURSELF... MAYBE YOU SHOULD GO HOME AND WATCH TV UNTIL YOU PASS OUT AT 2 AM... OR MAYBE YOU SHOULD TAKE CONTROL OF YOUR LIFE AND GRAB SOME OF THAT LOVE FOR YOURSELF.

FIG. 1 TYPICAL HAPPY COUPLE (SIMULATED) SURROUNDED BY FRIENDS AND WELL-WISHERS. CAN YOU SPOT YOURSELF IN THIS PICTURE?

MAYBE YOUR PROBLEM IS THAT LOVE IS AN ILLUSION
YIKES! LET'S LISTEN TO ONE EXPERIENCED SCIENTIST OF LOVE:

LOVE IS JUST A SIMPLE-MINDED LITTLE EUPHEMISM FOR A GRAB-BAG OF PRIMITIVE SEXUAL IMPULSES, UNRELENTING NEEDINESS, NEUROTIC ANXIETY, AND BRAIN-SQUEEZING SOCIAL PRESSURE. YOU'RE PUSHED TO COUPLE WITH YOUR SO-CALLED SOUL-MATE WITH ALL THE POETRY AND RAPTURE OF TWO SEA SLUGS ENCOUNTERING EACH OTHER ON THE BOTTOM OF THE OCEAN. AND I'M NOT JUST SAYING THIS BECAUSE MY GIRLFRIEND DUMPED ME THREE WEEKS AGO.

YOUR PROBLEM WITH LOVE -- A SMALL QUIZ
CHECK ANY OR ALL BOXES THAT DESCRIBE YOUR MENTAL STATE. THERE ARE NO RIGHT OR WRONG ANSWERS.
- ☐ LOVE IS PROFOUND ECSTASY.
- ☐ LOVE IS PROFOUND SUFFERING.
- ☐ LOVE IS MAGIC.
- ☐ LOVE IS A MAGIC TRICK.
- ☐ LOVE IS THE GREATEST THING IN LIFE.
- ☐ LOVE IS A PATHOLOGICAL ADDICTION.
- ☐ LOVE IS THE BEST.
- ☐ LOVE IS A SUBSTITUTE FOR THE STRUGGLE TOWARD SELF-FULFILLMENT.
- ☐ LOVE IS NEVER HAVING TO SAY YOU'RE SORRY.
- ☐ LOVE IS ALWAYS HAVING TO SAY YOU'RE SORRY.
- ☐ LOVE IS REAL
- ☐ LOVE IS A DELUSION.
- ☐ LOVE IS A DREAM.
- ☐ LOVE IS A NIGHTMARE.
- ☐ HELP ME.

LOVE SECRET #2
HE MAY BE RIGHT, BUT DON'T GO OUT WITH THAT GUY.

LIFE IN HELL

©1992 BY MATT GROENING KAUAI

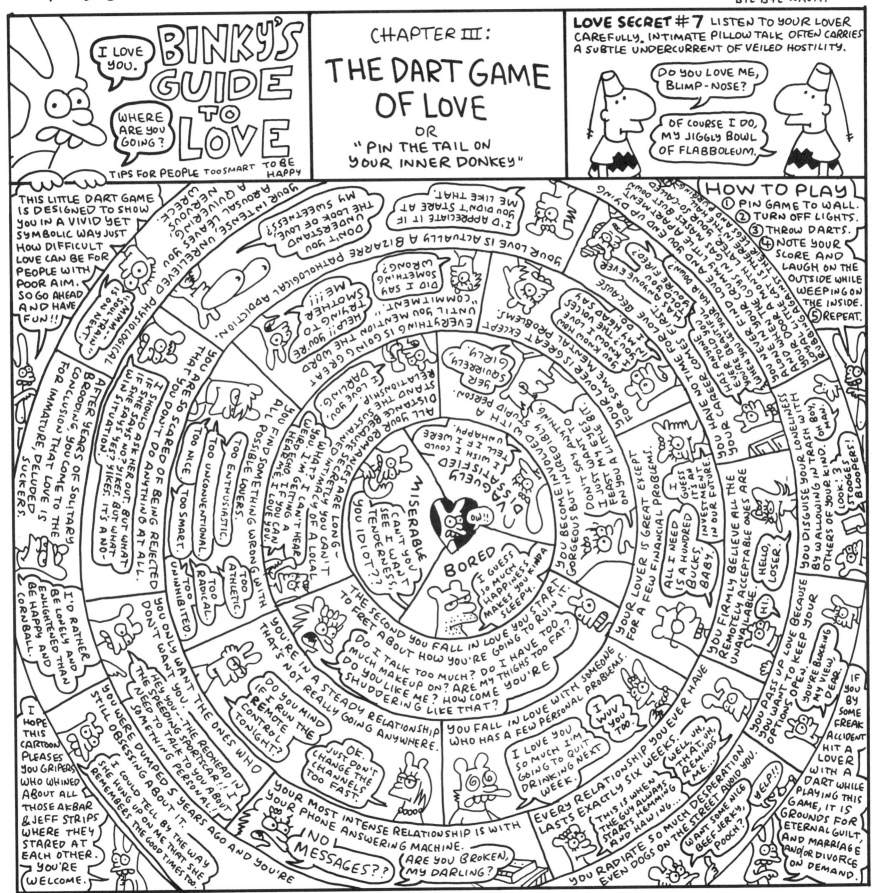

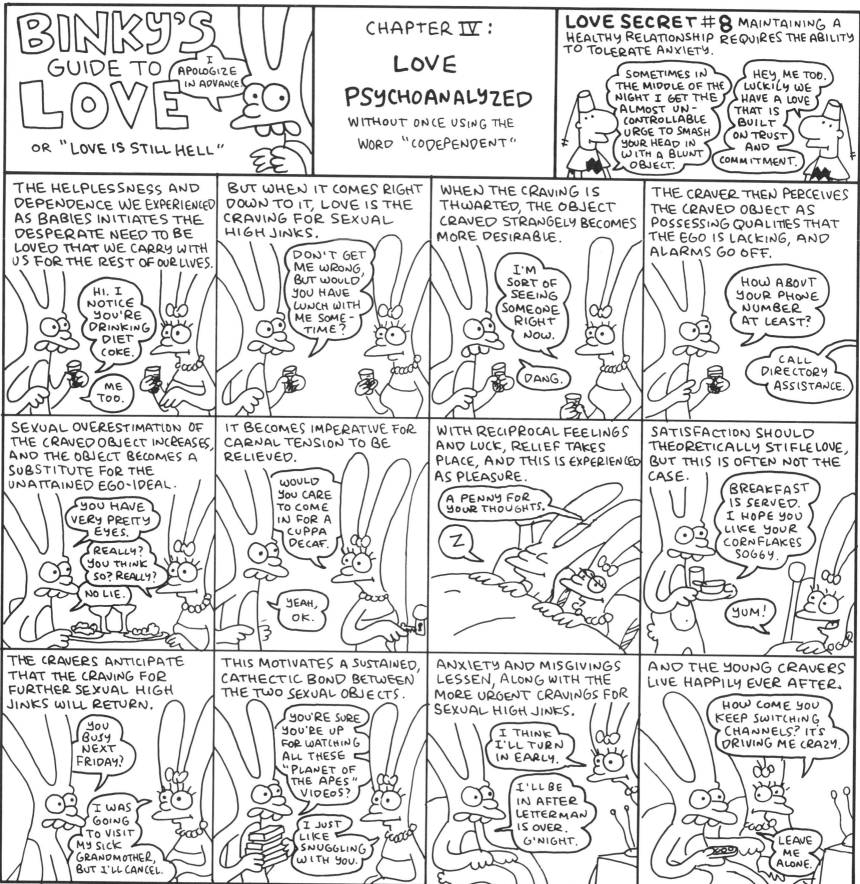

LIFE IN HELL

©1992 BY MATT GROENING

©1992
BY MATT GROENING

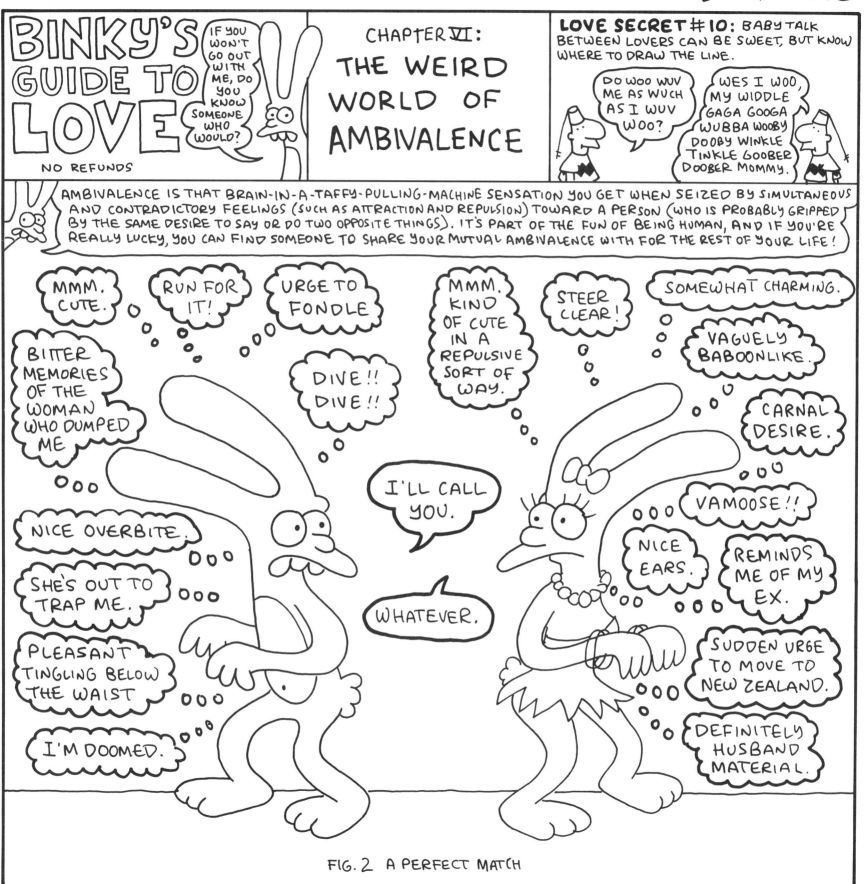

BINKY'S GUIDE TO LOVE

NO REFUNDS

IF YOU WON'T GO OUT WITH ME, DO YOU KNOW SOMEONE WHO WOULD?

CHAPTER VI:

THE WEIRD WORLD OF AMBIVALENCE

LOVE SECRET #10: BABY TALK BETWEEN LOVERS CAN BE SWEET, BUT KNOW WHERE TO DRAW THE LINE.

DO WOO WUV ME AS WUCH AS I WUV WOO?

WES I WOO, MY WIDDLE GAGA GOOGA WUBBA WOOBY DOOBY WINKLE TINKLE GOOBER DOOBER MOMMY.

AMBIVALENCE IS THAT BRAIN-IN-A-TAFFY-PULLING-MACHINE SENSATION YOU GET WHEN SEIZED BY SIMULTANEOUS AND CONTRADICTORY FEELINGS (SUCH AS ATTRACTION AND REPULSION) TOWARD A PERSON (WHO IS PROBABLY GRIPPED BY THE SAME DESIRE TO SAY OR DO TWO OPPOSITE THINGS). IT'S PART OF THE FUN OF BEING HUMAN, AND IF YOU'RE REALLY LUCKY, YOU CAN FIND SOMEONE TO SHARE YOUR MUTUAL AMBIVALENCE WITH FOR THE REST OF YOUR LIFE!

MMM. CUTE.

RUN FOR IT!

URGE TO FONDLE

MMM. KIND OF CUTE IN A REPULSIVE SORT OF WAY.

STEER CLEAR!

SOMEWHAT CHARMING.

VAGUELY BABOONLIKE.

BITTER MEMORIES OF THE WOMAN WHO DUMPED ME

DIVE!! DIVE!!

CARNAL DESIRE.

NICE OVERBITE.

I'LL CALL YOU.

VAMOOSE!!

SHE'S OUT TO TRAP ME.

WHATEVER.

NICE EARS.

REMINDS ME OF MY EX.

PLEASANT TINGLING BELOW THE WAIST

SUDDEN URGE TO MOVE TO NEW ZEALAND.

I'M DOOMED.

DEFINITELY HUSBAND MATERIAL.

FIG. 2 A PERFECT MATCH

©1992 BY MATT GROENING

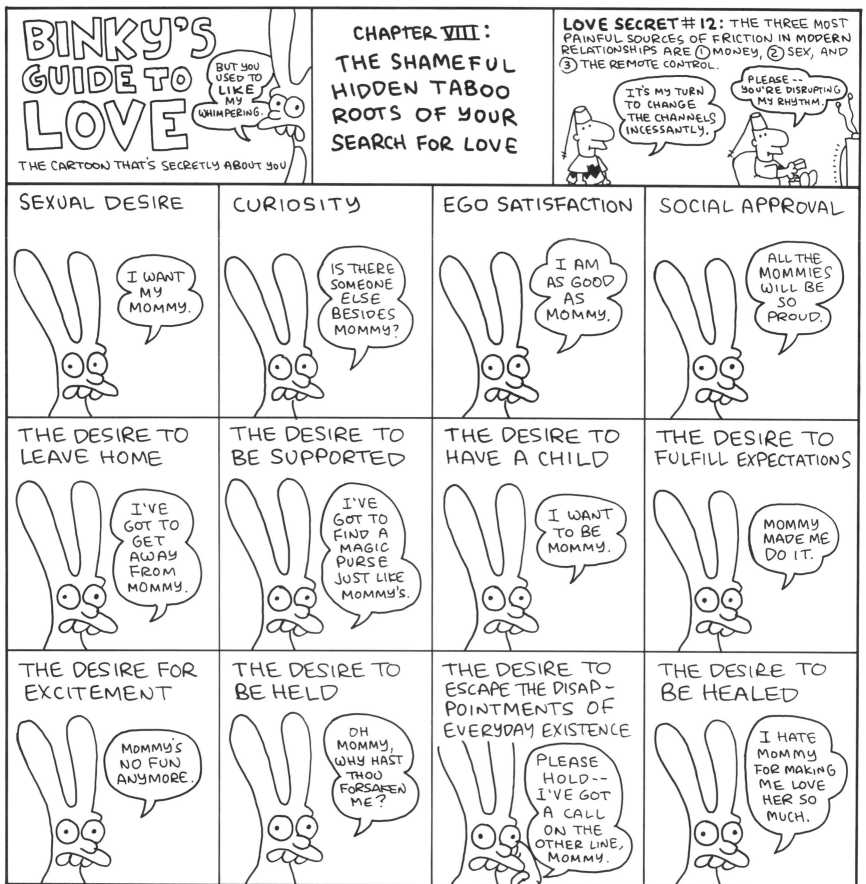

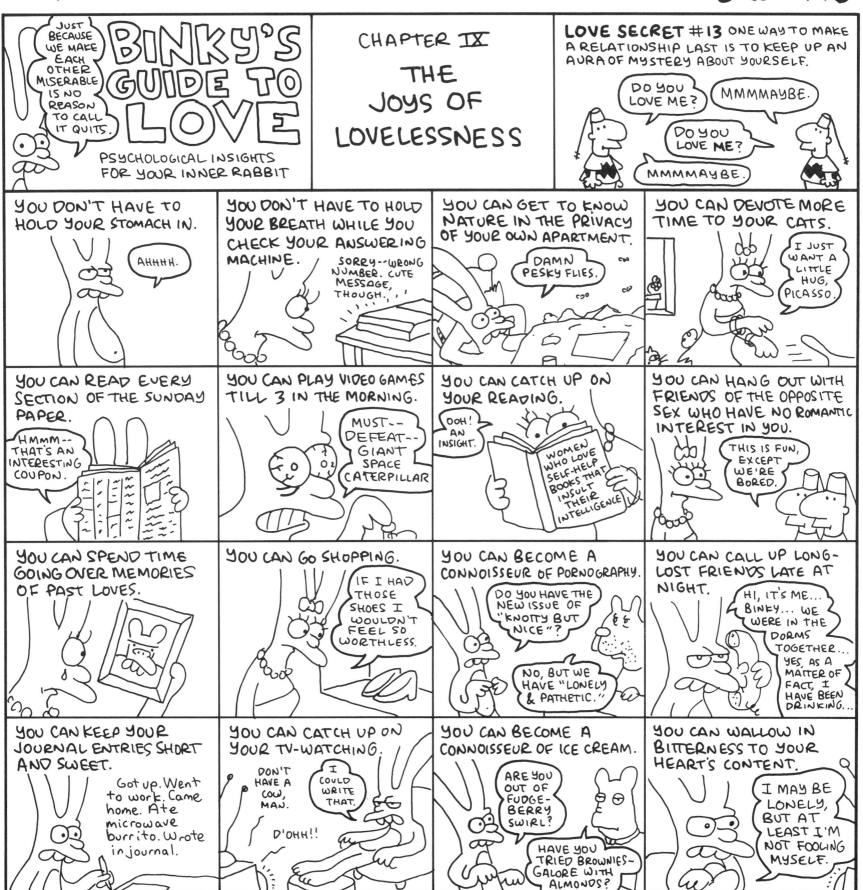

LIFE IN HELL

©1992 BY MATT GROENING

BINKY'S GUIDE TO LOVE

LOVE TIPS FOR THE UNLOVEABLE

WHEN YOU SAY YOU HATE ME IT MAKES ME THINK MAYBE YOU DON'T LOVE ME.

CHAPTER XI:

WHY YOU'RE SO SCREWED UP

THE BRIEFEST OF OVERVIEWS

LOVE SECRET #15 ONE OF THE JOYS OF TRUE LOVE IS GAZING INTO YOUR BELOVED'S EYES AND DISCOVERING NEW SOURCES OF BEAUTY AND DELIGHT.

A PENNY FOR YOUR THOUGHTS.

I WAS JUST NOTICING BOTH YOUR EYES ARE ON THE SAME SIDE OF YOUR NOSE.

ONE THING ABOUT YOUR SEEMINGLY FUTILE SEARCH FOR LOVE IS GUARANTEED: COMPLETE AND UTTER DREAD.

WAS THAT WOMAN IN THE CAFETERIA SMILING AT ME OR SNARLING AT ME?

NO MATTER HOW STABLE YOU THINK YOU ARE, WHEN IT COMES TO YOUR FRANTIC SEARCH FOR A LOVER, THE FACT IS THAT DEEP DOWN INSIDE YOU'RE A QUIVERING FOOL.

WHAT DID IT MEAN WHEN SHE LADLED ME THAT EXTRA CLAM CHOWDER?

MAYBE YOU'RE SOMEONE WHO LIVES A CREATIVE AND PRODUCTIVE LIFE, PRETENDING YOU AREN'T BOTHERED THAT YOU'RE A LOVELESS MUTANT.

WHY DID I SMACK MY LIPS AND QUIP "YUM-- CORNSTARCH"?

NO, IT DOESN'T BUG YOU A BIT THAT YOU'RE ALL ALONE IN THE BIG CITY EATING TASTELESS DINNER SALADS WITH ROCK-HARD CHERRY TOMATOES.

WHY DIDN'T SHE RESPOND WHEN I COMPLIMENTED HER HAIRNET?

NO, YOU'RE NOT SEETHING AT ALL THAT YOU'RE SURROUNDED BY HAPPY, SIMPERING COUPLES.

WHY DID SHE LADLE THE GUY BEHIND ME EXTRA CLAM CHOWDER TOO?

THEY THINK THEY'RE SUCH HOT STUFF WITH THEIR GIGGLING AND NUZZLING AND RICHLY VARIED, REGULAR SEX.

WHAT DID SHE MEAN WHEN SHE SAID "HAVE A NICE DAY"?

LOVE IS AGONY BECAUSE YOU KNOW YOU'RE GOING TO SCREW IT UP COMPLETELY AND END UP ALONE AGAIN, REJECTED AND HUMILIATED.

WHY DID SHE SHORT- CHANGE ME?

BUT MAYBE YOU CAN HARNESS YOUR SEETHING RAGE AND SPLITTING HEADACHES AND EMBITTERED LONELINESS AND THROBBING SEXUAL FRUSTRATION INTO SOMETHING SWEET AND POSITIVE.

I MUST HAVE THAT BEWITCHING LITTLE TEMPTRESS.

IF YOU DON'T SUCCEED AT FIRST, FAIL AGAIN.

UH, COULD YOU-- WOULD YOU-- COULD I-- ER-- HAVE SOME MORE TARTAR SAUCE?

SURE. THAT'LL BE 35¢.

LIFE IN HELL

©1992 BY MATT GROENING

BINKY'S GUIDE TO LOVE

TEMPORARY RELIEF FOR THE ROMANTICALLY TORMENTED

EVEN IF YOU DON'T LOVE ME, I THINK I HAVE ENOUGH LOVE FOR THE BOTH OF US.

CHAPTER XII:
9 COMMON RUTS

LOVE SECRET #16: BEFORE BEGINNING AN ARGUMENT, LOVERS SHOULD AGREE ON THE GROUND RULES SO THAT BOTH PARTNERS CAN BE SATISFIED.

I THINK WE SHOULD SAY TERRIBLY HURTFUL THINGS THAT WE'LL LATER REGRET.

I THINK WE SHOULD SCREECH AT EACH OTHER UNTIL WE'RE BOTH COMPLETELY HOARSE.

OK. / OK.

YOU'RE SO AFRAID OF LOSING LOVE THAT YOU NEVER GET STARTED AT ALL.

HI. / HI! / OH FERGET IT.

LOVE MAKES YOU CRAZY, NOT HAPPY.

JUST BECAUSE YOU FEEL LONELY, UNHAPPY, HEARTBROKEN, AND DEPRESSED DOESN'T MEAN YOU'RE A LOSER.

WHAT WAS THE LAST WORD YOU SAID?

LOSER.

YOU'RE RIGHT. I AM A LOSER.

YOU PLUNGE INTO EVERY ROMANCE WITH ABANDON, ONLY TO EXPERIENCE EXTREME REGRET.

I SAID, WHAT'S FER BREAKFAST?

YOU ONLY GO OUT WITH PEOPLE WHO ARE UNSUITABLE FOR YOU.

YOU SEE, THE SPOTTED OWL IS JUST A SYMBOL FOR THE WHOLE ECOSYSTEM.

ECO-WHUT?

YOU FIND SOMETHING WRONG WITH EVERYBODY.

YOU DEALPHABETIZED MY CD COLLECTION!!

I'M AFRAID THIS RELATIONSHIP IS OVER.

YOU ALWAYS GET DUMPED JUST AS THINGS ARE STARTING TO GET INTERESTING.

THAT WAS THE MOST INCREDIBLE SEX OF MY ENTIRE LIFE.

YES, BUT THINGS JUST AREN'T WORKING OUT.

YOUR LOVER WON'T MAKE A COMMITMENT, AND YOU'RE TOO SCARED TO DO ANYTHING ABOUT IT.

HAVE YOU EVER THOUGHT ABOUT MARRIAGE?

HEY, DON'T RUIN A GOOD THING.

LOOK! A NEW COMIC-BOOK STORE!

YOU CAN'T MAKE A COMMITMENT BECAUSE YOU MIGHT BE MAKING A HORRIBLE MISTAKE.

I'M LONELY AND BORED AND WORRIED AND FRUSTRATED BUT IT'S NOT SO BAD WHEN THERE'S SOMETHING GOOD ON.

YOU ONLY DESIRE THE ONES WHO DON'T DESIRE YOU.

WOULD YOU CARE TO DANCE?

NOT REALLY.

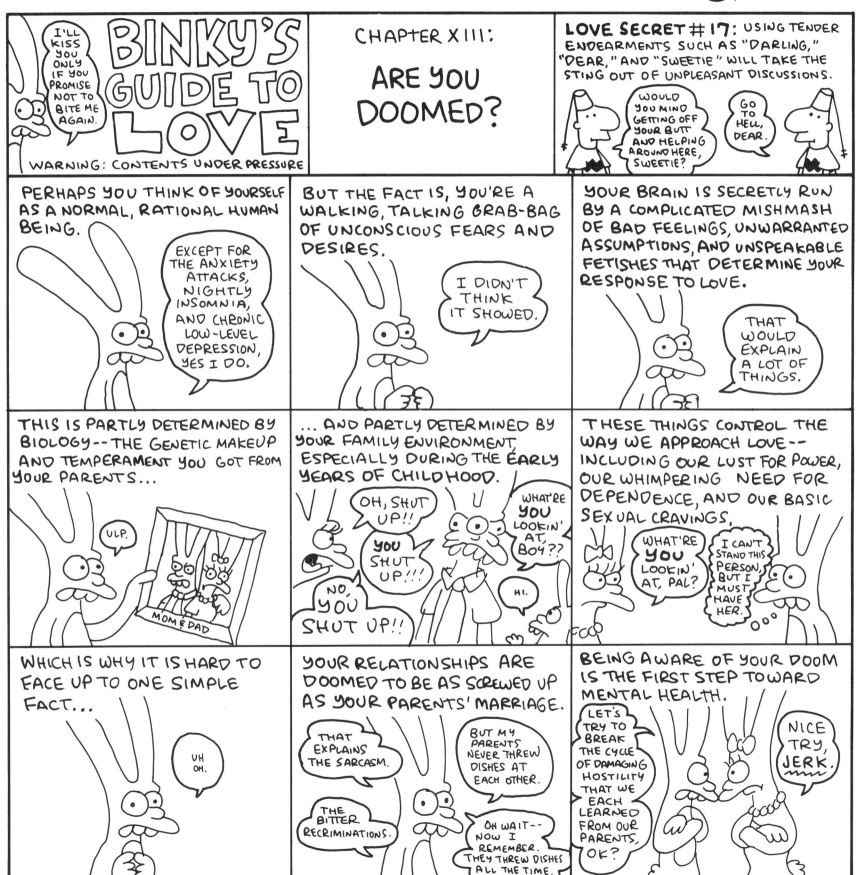

©1992 BY MATT GROENING

©1992 BY MATT GROENING

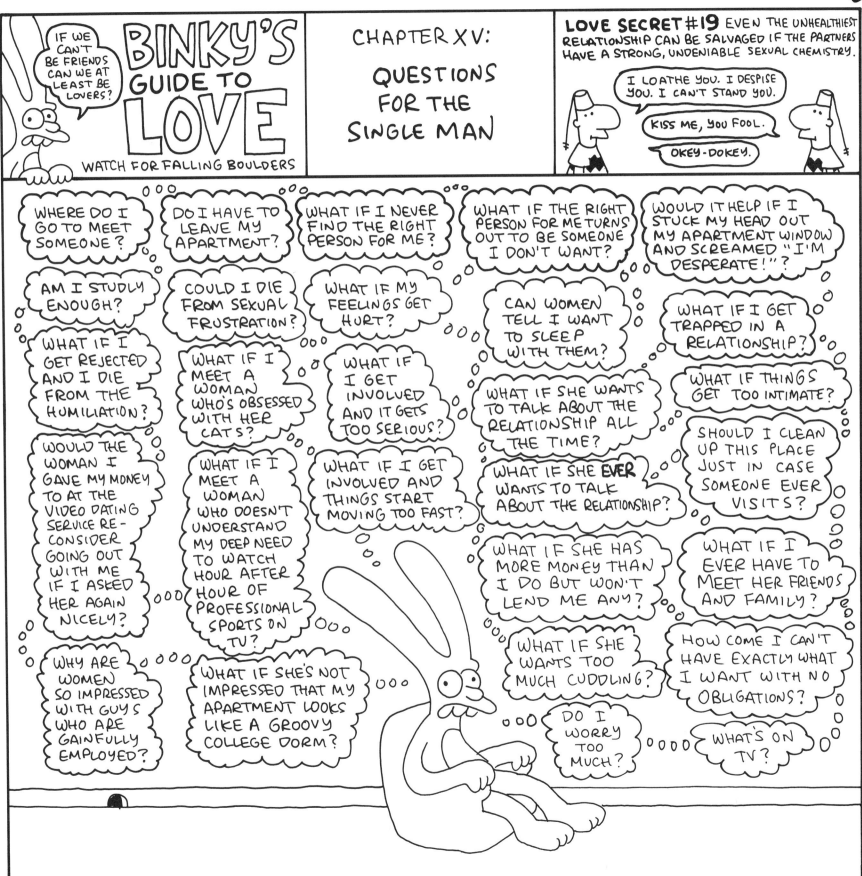

© 1992 BY MATT GROENING

LIFE IN HELL

© 1992 BY MATT GROENING

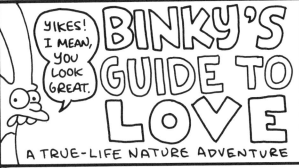

BINKY'S GUIDE TO LOVE

A TRUE-LIFE NATURE ADVENTURE

YIKES! I MEAN, YOU LOOK GREAT.

CHAPTER XIX:

DARE A WOMAN MAKE THE FIRST MOVE?

LOVE SECRET # 22: WHEN YOU SENSE YOU ARE LOSING A HEATED ARGUMENT, SUDDENLY SAY THE FOUR MAGIC WORDS THAT WILL LEAVE YOUR LOVER UTTERLY FRUSTRATED.

LET'S AGREE TO DISAGREE.

SURE, THE PROSPECT OF BREAKING THE LONG-STANDING SOCIAL TABOO AGAINST MAKING THE FIRST MOVE GOES AGAINST EVERYTHING YOUR BARBIE DOLL EVER TAUGHT YOU. BUT REMEMBER: IF YOU ARE UNWILLING TO CHOOSE AMONG THE JERKS, YOU WILL BE LIMITED TO CHOOSING FROM THE JERKS WHO CHOOSE YOU. SO RELAX, BE YOURSELF, AND GO CRAZY.

© 1992 BY MATT GROENING

BINKY'S GUIDE TO LOVE
"YOU BREAK IT, YOU BUY IT"

BUT I THOUGHT WE HAD AN UNSPOKEN AGREEMENT.

CHAPTER XX:

QUESTIONABLE OPENING LINES

LOVE SECRET #23: YOUR PARTNER'S ATTEMPTS TO BE NICE CAN BE DEFEATED EFFORTLESSLY JUST BY REPEATING THE TEN MAGIC WORDS.

YOU'RE JUST SAYING WHAT YOU THINK I WANT TO HEAR.

DON'T GET ME WRONG, BUT WOULD YOU CARE TO DO THE HOKEY POKEY?

I INSIST YOU COME TO MY POETRY READING.

I CAN TELL YOU HATE GETTING OLD AND WRINKLED AS MUCH AS I DO.

PLEASE PARDON THE SMELL OF INSECTICIDE, BUT YOU WOULDN'T BELIEVE THE DAY I HAD.

I DON'T MEAN TO SOUND IMMODEST, BUT I AM GOD'S GIFT TO WOMEN.

IS THERE SOMEONE FOLLOWING ME?

DO YOU BELIEVE IN OBSESSIVE LOVE AT FIRST SIGHT?

MY CAR BATTERY IS DEAD. YOU GOT ANY SPARE JUMPER CABLES? BY THE WAY, YOU'RE BEAUTIFUL.

DO YOU KNOW HOW MANY CONTAMINANTS THE FDA ALLOWS IN THAT SNACK YOU'RE EATING?

I HAVE EVERY EPISODE OF "STAR TREK" ON TAPE. YOU BUSY SATURDAY?

ARE YOU A LOST SOUL TOO?

YOU MAY RECOGNIZE ME FROM MY INFOMERCIALS.

CAN I TELL YOU A SHOCKING PERSONAL SECRET?

♪ SOMEONE'S GOT A RUN IN HER PANTYHOSE ♫

LET ME GIVE YOU MY PHILOSOPHY IN A NUTSHELL.

HI. MY NAME IS BINKY, BUT YOU CAN CALL ME BY MY NICKNAME: SAFE-SEX CHARLIE.

LIFE IN HELL

©1992 BY MATT GROENING

BINKY'S GUIDE TO LOVE

NOT FOR THE SQUEAMISH

DOES THIS MEAN YOU'RE NOT MY LITTLE CREAM-PUFF ANYMORE?

CHAPTER XXI:
MORE QUESTIONABLE OPENING LINES

LOVE SECRET #24: IT'S EASY TO SAY THINGS THAT WILL INFURIATE YOUR LOVER. BUT IF YOU ARE CREATIVE, YOU CAN COME UP WITH REMARKS THAT WILL CAUSE A BRAIN-IMPLODING FRENZY OF ANGER AND AMUSEMENT.

IT'D JUST BE A WASTE OF TIME EXPLAINING IT TO YOU.

I GENERALLY HATE WOMEN, BUT YOU'RE DIFFERENT.

I'M JUST A BIG OLD LONELY GRIZZLY BEAR.

WOULD YOU MIND A LITTLE CONSTRUCTIVE CRITICISM?

HAVE YOU EVER PUNCHED OUT YOUR THERAPIST? I'M PROUD TO SAY I HAVE.

MY MAIN FAULT IS I HAVE A TENDENCY TO LIE.

DO YOU CONSTANTLY CRAVE CHILI LIKE I DO?

COULD YOU POSSIBLY RUB THIS OINTMENT ON MY RASH?

I BET YOU'VE NEVER MET A REPUBLICAN NUDIST BEFORE.

HOW WOULD YOU LIKE TO HELP ME EDIT MY GRANT PROPOSAL?

I'M SICK OF PASSION. I'M JUST LOOKING FOR SOMEONE TO PLAY PICTIONARY WITH.

I COLLECT COMIC BOOKS, BUT I'M NOT ONE OF THOSE NERDS WHO COLLECTS COMIC BOOKS.

I NEED A **BIG HUG.**

I HOPE MOTHER LIKES YOU AS MUCH AS I DO.

WILL YOU BE MY BIBLE BUDDY?

PERHAPS YOU RECOGNIZE ME FROM MY ADULT MOVIES.

I BELIEVE YOU CAN'T LOVE ANYONE ELSE UNTIL YOU LOVE YOURSELF. AND QUITE FRANKLY, I'M IN LOVE WITH MYSELF.

LIFE IN HELL

©1992 BY MATT GROENING

BINKY'S GUIDE TO LOVE

BUT HOW CAN I BE SUPPORTIVE IF YOU WON'T LET ME CONTROL YOU?

DO NOT USE IF SEAL IS BROKEN

CHAPTER XXIII:

THE MAGICAL FOOLISHNESS OF LOVE

LOVE SECRET #26: NOT FEELING UNHAPPY ENOUGH? TRY POUTING UNTIL YOUR LOVER ASKS WHAT'S WRONG, THEN SAY THE FOLLOWING IN A WHINY, HURT VOICE:

IF I TELL YOU WHAT I WANT AND THEN YOU DO IT, IT DOESN'T COUNT BECAUSE I HAD TO TELL YOU.

NOBODY IN THE HISTORY OF THE WORLD HAS EVER FELT LIKE US.

LIFE IN HELL

©1992 By Matt Groening

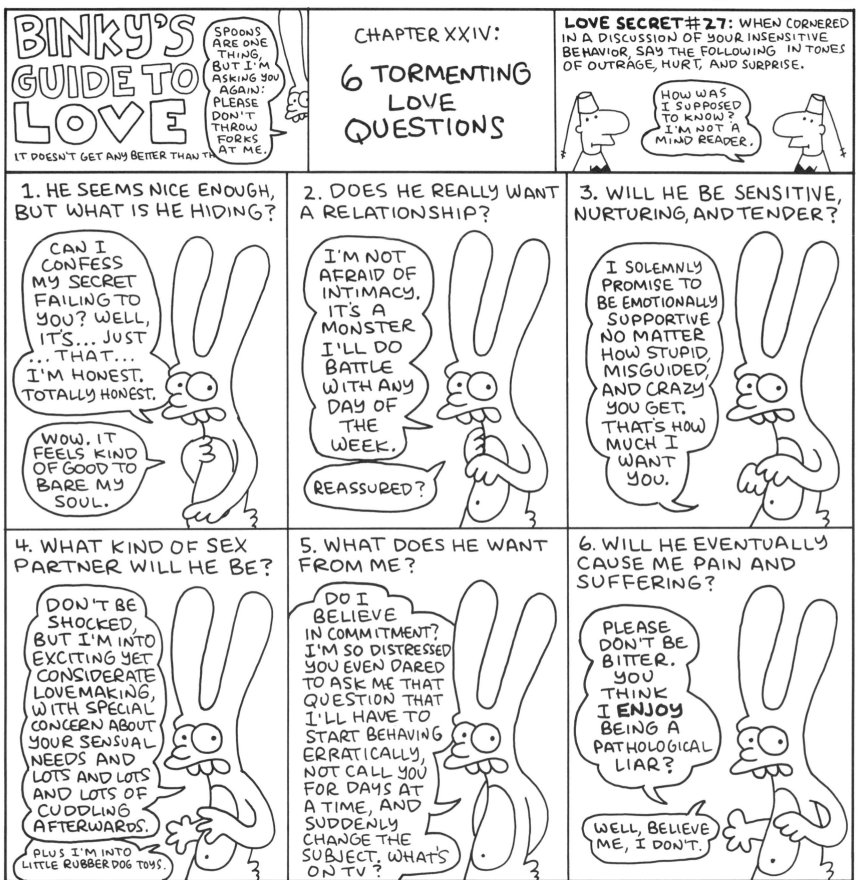

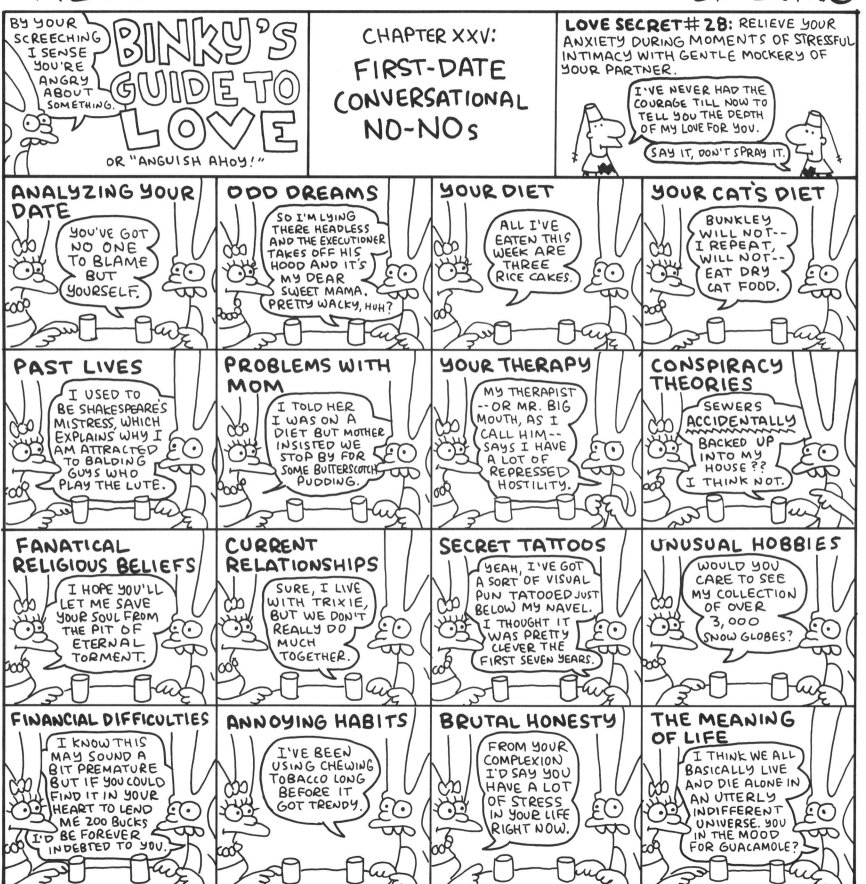

©1993 BY MATT GROENING

LIFE IN HELL

©1993 BY MATT GROENING

HOW WOULD YOU DESCRIBE OUR RELATIONSHIP?

RAGING, SCREAMING FIGHTS.

LONG, SULLEN SILENCES.

VICIOUS NAME-CALLING.

BITTER RECRIMINATIONS.

GUT-WRENCHING HOSTILITY.

SELFISHNESS AND INSENSITIVITY.

LOUSY FOOD AND A PIGSTY OF AN APARTMENT.

PETTY BICKERING.

DOOR-SLAMMING AND DISH-SMASHING.

JOYLESSNESS.

NUMBNESS.

SEETHING ANGER.

A FEELING OF UTTER HOPLESSNESS.

RANDOM MOMENTS OF BIZARRE, ARBITRARY TENDERNESS THAT SOMEHOW KEEP US GOING.

©1989 BY
MATT
GROENING

LIFE IN HELL

©1990 BY MATT GROENING

©1989 BY MATT GROENING

©1992 BY Matt GROENING

© 1989 BY MATT GROENING

SECRETS OF THE CREATIVE

CREATIVE TYPE	SECRET FEAR	SECRET PAST	SECRET THRILL	SECRET AMBITION	SECRET SHAME
ROCK CRITIC	MAYBE ROCK & ROLL ISN'T HERE TO STAY	SURLY RECORD-STORE CLERK	TELLING IMPRESSIVE STORIES TO YOUNGER ROCK CRITICS	TO STRANGLE A NEWSPAPER EDITOR WITH BARE HANDS	MADE MORE MONEY AS A SURLY RECORD-STORE CLERK
COMMERCIAL ARTIST	MAYBE MY ILLUSTRATIONS WILL NEVER HANG IN ART MUSEUMS	PROMISING ART STUDENT	DEPOSITING PAYCHECKS	TO STRANGLE AN ART DIRECTOR WITH BARE HANDS	SALIVATES AT SIGHT OF OWN AIRBRUSHED HAMBURGERS
RADIO DJ	MAYBE THIS ISN'T SO GLAMOROUS AFTER ALL	TEEN-FAIR LIP-SYNC CONTEST WINNER	MAKING VOICE SOUND DECEPTIVELY DEEP AND CONFIDENT	TO STRANGLE A PROGRAM DIRECTOR WITH BARE HANDS	STEALS OTHER DJs' RECORDS
AD COPYWRITER	MAYBE MY BRAIN IS SLOWLY DEFLATING	COLLEGE SHORT-STORY CONTEST WINNER	MAKING LITTLE JOKEY ITEMS FOR THE OFFICE BULLETIN BOARD	TO STRANGLE AN AD DIRECTOR, A CLIENT, AND SELF WITH BARE HANDS	HAS LEARNED TO ENJOY THINKING UP SLOGANS ABOUT BEEF-A-RONI
CARTOONIST	MAYBE THIS IS NOT THE MOST IMPORTANT WAY TO SPEND MY EXISTENCE	COMPULSIVE DOODLER	GETTING PAID TO ANNOY OTHERS	NOT TO BE STRANGLED	SHAMELESS

LIFE IN HELL

©1992 BY MATT GROENING

EXPLAIN FAMILY VALUES.

GOOD VS. EVIL.

GOD VS. THE GODLESS.

A RELIGIOUS WAR FOR THE SOUL OF AMERICA.

HATRED OF HOMOSEXUALS.

RACE-BAITING.

HILLARY-BASHING.

THE WALTONS VS. THE SIMPSONS.

ANTI-FEMINISM.

ANTI-CHILDREN'S RIGHTS.

PRO-GUN.

ANTI-ABORTION.

PRO-WAR.

OH, I GET IT.

MANSON FAMILY VALUES.

41

LIFE IN HELL

©1992 BY MATT GROENING

LIFE IN HELL

©1992 BY MATT GROENING

MAYBE THE REPUBLICANS ARE RIGHT.

MAYBE MY ALTERNATIVE LIFESTYLE IS DEPRAVED.

MAYBE I AM SO VILE I DON'T DESERVE EQUAL RIGHTS.

WHAT ARE YOU TALKING ABOUT?

YOU CAN'T FALL FOR THE ANTISEXUAL DIATRIBES OF JOYLESS PRIGS.

SEX IS ZEST AND EXCITEMENT, FUN AND FOOLISHNESS.

WHY DO YOU THINK THEY CALL IT CARNAL DELIGHT?

YOU MUSTN'T BE DIVIDED AGAINST YOURSELF, TRYING TO BE SOMETHING YOU'RE NOT.

SEX IS FUN.

YOU ARE WHO YOU ARE.

YOU HAVE NOTHING TO BE ASHAMED OF.

DON'T LET ANYONE JUDGE YOU FOR YOUR DESIRES.

I AM SEXUALLY AROUSED BY DAN QUAYLE.

THAT'S DISGUSTING.

LIFE IN HELL

© 1989 BY MATT GROENING

WOW.

GETTING YOUR HEAD CHOPPED OFF BY A GUILLOTINE WOULD BE WEIRD.

WHAT WOULD BE GOING THROUGH YOUR MIND WHEN YOU GOT CLAMPED IN?

WOULD YOU SQUIRM OR WOULD YOU JUST SIT THERE?

WOULD YOU YELL OR WOULD YOU JUST KEEP YOUR MOUTH SHUT?

WHAT WOULD YOUR LAST THOUGHTS BE AS THE BLADE STARTED TO FALL?

BONGO! QUIT DAYDREAMING AND PAY ATTENTION.

WOW.

©1993 BY MATT GROENING

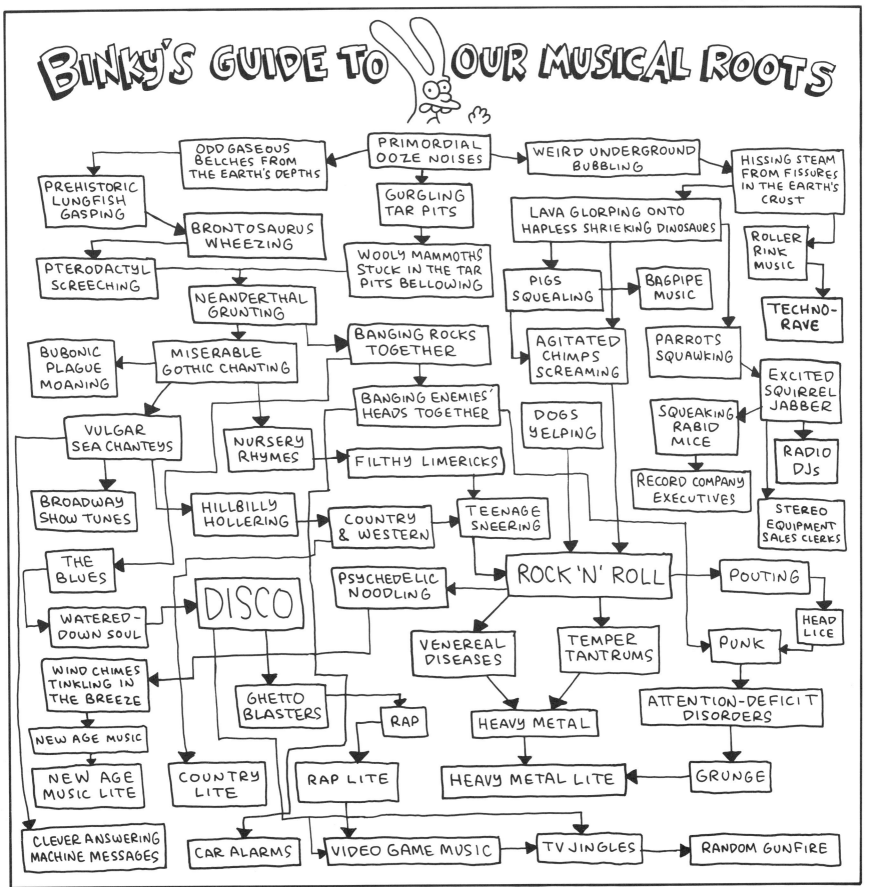

BINKY'S GUIDE TO OUR MUSICAL ROOTS

LIFE IN HELL

©1992 BY MATT GROENING

THEY'RE LETTING GAYS IN THE MILITARY NOW.

YEE HAW!

FORWARD MARCH!

BE ALL THAT YOU CAN BE!

HUP TWO THREE FO!

WE'RE LOOKING FOR A FEW GOOD MEN!

I WANT YOU!

WE'RE IN THE ARMY NOW!

REST AND RECREATION!

CRUISIN' FOR A BRUISIN'!

ROCK AND ROLL!

OPPORTUNITIES FOR ADVANCEMENT!

WOO HOO!

WOO.

HOO.

WHAT WERE WE THINKING?

© 1993 BY MATT GROENING

©1989 BY MATT GROENING

LIFE IN HELL

©1989 BY MATT GROENING
* THANKS TO SANDRA ROBINSON

KIDS WANT TO KNOW

DO DOG MOVIE-STARS KNOW THEY'RE FAMOUS?

WHAT DID PEOPLE DO AT NIGHT BEFORE THERE WAS TV?

DO ANTS HAVE SOULS?

WHAT DOES HUMAN FLESH TASTE LIKE?

WHAT IF THE OPPOSITE SEX ARE ALL REALLY MARTIANS?

WHO INVENTED THE IDEA OF STICKING YOUR GUM UNDER THE TABLE IN RESTAURANTS?

DON'T PLANTS GET BORED JUST SITTING THERE?

DO SLUGS DREAM?

DO CARS FEEL PAIN WHEN THEY CRASH?

WHAT IF EVERYONE IN THE WORLD IS A ROBOT EXCEPT ME?

ARE STARVING CHILDREN ON TV REALLY REAL?

IF CATS THOUGHT THEY COULD GET AWAY WITH IT, WOULD THEY MURDER US ALL IN OUR SLEEP?

DID PEOPLE IN THE OLD DAYS REALIZE HOW CORNY THEY WERE?

HOW DO YOU REALLY KNOW FOR SURE WHEN A QUESTION HAS BEEN ANSWERED?

WHY **CAN'T** I HAVE ANOTHER COOKIE?

51

LIFE IN HELL

©1993 BY MATT GROENING

NOTHING YOU SAY WILL MAKE ME SUCCUMB TO YOUR SEDUCTIVE CARNAL WILES.

WE'RE JUST A COUPLE OF FROLICSOME LITTLE SMUT-SQUIRRELS.

NOPE.

WE'RE JUST A COUPLE OF PLAYFUL LITTLE PASSION-DUCKS.

NO WAY.

WE'RE JUST A COUPLE OF SPORTY LITTLE LUST-WEASELS.

NOPE.

WE'RE JUST A COUPLE OF JOYFUL LITTLE PERVO-GOATS.

NICE TRY.

WE'RE JUST A COUPLE OF MISCHIEVOUS LITTLE TOUCH-MONKEYS.

NOPE.

WE'RE JUST A COUPLE OF FRIVOLITY-LOVING EROTO-HAMSTERS.

FORGET IT.

WE'RE JUST A COUPLE OF FRISKY LITTLE BOUNCE-BUNNIES.

DAMN.

LIFE IN HELL

©1989 BY MATT GROENING

HOW TO KEEP FROM EXPLODING WITH RAGE

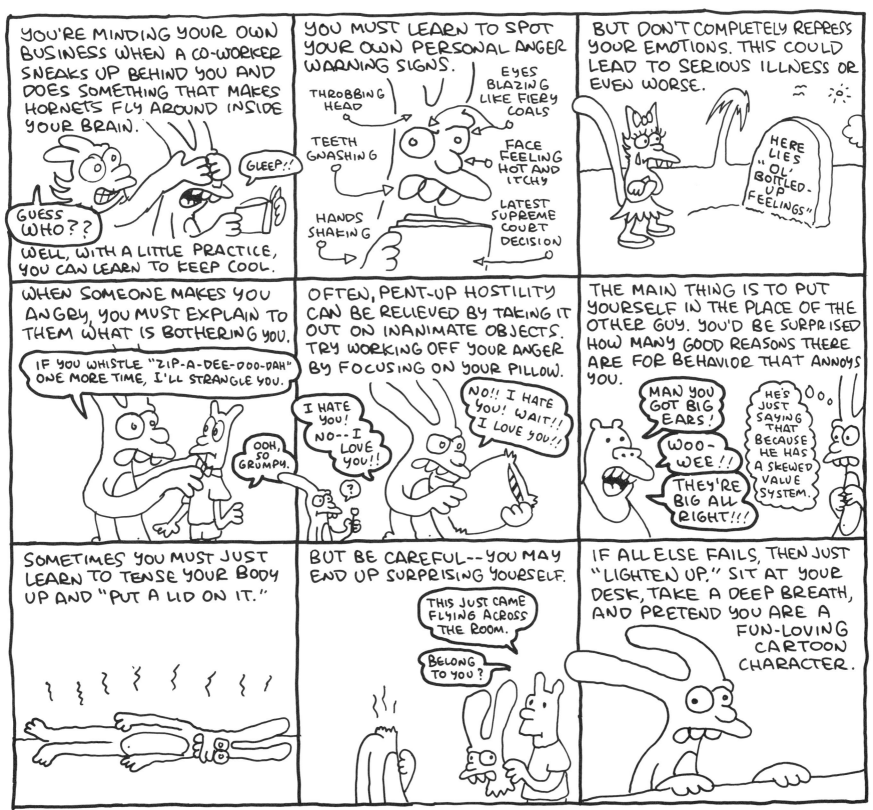

YOU'RE MINDING YOUR OWN BUSINESS WHEN A CO-WORKER SNEAKS UP BEHIND YOU AND DOES SOMETHING THAT MAKES HORNETS FLY AROUND INSIDE YOUR BRAIN.

GLEEP!!

GUESS WHO??

WELL, WITH A LITTLE PRACTICE, YOU CAN LEARN TO KEEP COOL.

YOU MUST LEARN TO SPOT YOUR OWN PERSONAL ANGER WARNING SIGNS.

THROBBING HEAD

TEETH GNASHING

HANDS SHAKING

EYES BLAZING LIKE FIERY COALS

FACE FEELING HOT AND ITCHY

LATEST SUPREME COURT DECISION

BUT DON'T COMPLETELY REPRESS YOUR EMOTIONS. THIS COULD LEAD TO SERIOUS ILLNESS OR EVEN WORSE.

HERE LIES "OL' BOTTLED-UP FEELINGS"

WHEN SOMEONE MAKES YOU ANGRY, YOU MUST EXPLAIN TO THEM WHAT IS BOTHERING YOU.

IF YOU WHISTLE "ZIP-A-DEE-DOO-DAH" ONE MORE TIME, I'LL STRANGLE YOU.

OOH, SO GRUMPY.

OFTEN, PENT-UP HOSTILITY CAN BE RELIEVED BY TAKING IT OUT ON INANIMATE OBJECTS. TRY WORKING OFF YOUR ANGER BY FOCUSING ON YOUR PILLOW.

I HATE YOU! NO--I LOVE YOU!!

NO!! I HATE YOU! WAIT!! I LOVE YOU!!

THE MAIN THING IS TO PUT YOURSELF IN THE PLACE OF THE OTHER GUY. YOU'D BE SURPRISED HOW MANY GOOD REASONS THERE ARE FOR BEHAVIOR THAT ANNOYS YOU.

MAN YOU GOT BIG EARS!

WOO-WEE!!

THEY'RE BIG ALL RIGHT!!!

HE'S JUST SAYING THAT BECAUSE HE HAS A SKEWED VALUE SYSTEM.

SOMETIMES YOU MUST JUST LEARN TO TENSE YOUR BODY UP AND "PUT A LID ON IT."

BUT BE CAREFUL--YOU MAY END UP SURPRISING YOURSELF.

THIS JUST CAME FLYING ACROSS THE ROOM.

BELONG TO YOU?

IF ALL ELSE FAILS, THEN JUST "LIGHTEN UP." SIT AT YOUR DESK, TAKE A DEEP BREATH, AND PRETEND YOU ARE A FUN-LOVING CARTOON CHARACTER.

LIFE IN HELL

© 1993 BY MATT GROENING

THE RETURN OF THE DINOSAUR POP-UP BOOK
FEATURING
DAD — ABE

BUH. BUH. BUH.

BALL?

BOTTLE?

BOOK?

BUH!

SURE, I'LL READ YOU A BOOK. GO GET ONE.

BUT PLEASE GET SOMETHING ELSE BESIDES THE DINOSAUR POP-UP BOOK, PLEASE.

D'OHH.

IN THE MANNER OF HOMER SIMPSON

POP-UP DINOSAUR BOOK

THIS IS A PICTURE OF A STEGOSAURUS WITH ITS HEAD RIPPED OFF.

WUZZAT?

A HEADLESS STEGOSAURUS.

WUZZAT?

HEADLESS STEGOSAURUS.

AND HERE WE HAVE A PTERODACTYL WITH BOTH ITS WINGS TORN OFF.

WUZZAT?

WELL, THAT'S HIS HEAD, BUT DON'T—

WUZZAT?

THAT'S THE PTERODACTYL'S HEAD YOU JUST RIPPED OUT.

THERE'S NOT EVEN A DINOSAUR ON THIS PAGE.

WUZZAT?

THAT'S DRIED GLUE WHERE THE DINOSAUR USED TO BE.

IN FACT, ALL THE REST OF THE DINO-SAURS IN THE BOOK HAVE BEEN RIPPED OUT.

WUZZAT?

AGAIN, THAT'S DRIED GLUE.

BUH! BUH!

BUH! BUH!

OK, GET ANOTHER BOOK.

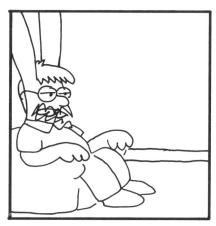

D'OHH.

IN THE MANNER OF HOMER SIMPSON

POP-UP DINOSAUR BOOK

LIFE IN HELL

©1993 BY MATT GROENING

LET'S FIGHT TO THE DEATH.

OK. BUT FIRST WE NEED TO GET RILED UP.

YOU'RE CRUISIN' FOR A BRUISIN'.

YOU'RE BLEATIN' FOR A BEATIN'.

YOU'RE FLIRTIN' FOR A HURTIN'!

YOU'RE CROAKIN' FOR A CHOKIN'.

YOU'RE GROANIN' FOR A STONIN'.

YOU'RE SKIPPIN' FOR A WHIPPIN'.

YOU'RE GRUBBIN' FOR A DRUBBIN'.

YOU'RE MUMBLIN' FOR A TUMBLIN'.

YOU'RE BOUNCIN' FOR A POUNCIN'.

YOU'RE SHOUTIN' FOR ASSAULTIN'.

YOU'RE SHUFFLIN' FOR A SCUFFLIN'.

YOU'RE CROONIN' FOR A HARPOONIN'.

YOU'RE STRUTTIN' FOR A GUTTIN'!

YOU'RE SQUIRMISH FOR A SKIRMISH.

YOU'RE CLOWNIN' FOR A DROWNIN'.

YOU'RE TOTTERIN' FOR A SLAUGHTERIN'.

YOU'RE ANGLIN' FOR A STRANGLIN'.

YOU'RE FLOATIN' FOR A SLIT-THROATIN'.

I'M OUTTA RHYMES.

ME TOO.

DAMN. WE WERE SO CLOSE.

©1990 BY MATT GROENING

©1990
BY MATT
GROENING

LIFE IN HELL

©1993 BY MATT GROENING

NO! WE MUSTN'T!

I AGREE. THIS IS WRONG.

IT'S A SIN.

IT'S DEPRAVED.

I AM FILLED WITH SHAME.

I'M MORTIFIED.

I'M CONSUMED WITH FEELINGS OF SELF-LOATHING.

I'M LOWER THAN A COMMON SEWER DOG.

I HATE MYSELF.

I MORE THAN HATE MYSELF.

I'M PURE FILTH.

I'M A PIECE OF FILTH STUCK TO THE BOTTOM OF A PIECE OF FILTH.

SO WHAT DO WE DO NEXT?

© 1989 BY MATT GROENING

LIFE IN HELL

HOW TO CHEER UP A DISGRUNTLED NEW MOTHER

A SAD BUT TRUE STORY

©1993 BY MATT GROENING

LIFE IN HELL

©1993 BY MATT GROENING

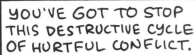

BOYS, BOYS, BOYS!

YOU'VE GOT TO STOP THIS DESTRUCTIVE CYCLE OF HURTFUL CONFLICT.

LET'S BEGIN THE HEALING PROCESS BY BEGINNING EACH SENTENCE WITH "RIGHT NOW I FEEL."

RIGHT NOW I FEEL HURT THAT THERE'S SO MUCH BLAMING IN OUR RELATIONSHIP.

GOOD.

RIGHT NOW I FEEL HURT WHEN I'M NOT UNDERSTOOD.

NICELY PUT.

RIGHT NOW I FEEL HURT THAT I DON'T KNOW WHAT THE HELL YOU'RE TALKING ABOUT.

HMM.

RIGHT NOW I FEEL HURT THAT YOU DON'T UNDERSTAND THE DEPTH OF MY CONTEMPT FOR YOU.

CAREFUL NOW.

RIGHT NOW I FEEL HURT THAT YOU DON'T REALIZE HOW MUCH I HATE YOUR LOUSY GUTS.

OH MY.

RIGHT NOW I FEEL HURT THAT I HAVE TO LOOK AT YOUR UGLY FACE.

THIS IS NOT--

RIGHT NOW I FEEL HURT THAT I HAVE TO RESTRAIN MYSELF FROM STRANGLING YOU.

PLEASE, YOU MUST--

RIGHT NOW I FEEL HURT THAT I'M GOING TO HAVE TO SMASH YOUR HEAD IN.

NOW, NOW, THAT'S NOT--

RIGHT NOW I FEEL HURT THAT YOU'RE GOING TO FORCE ME TO BEAT THE LIVING DAYLIGHTS OUT OF YOU.

OH!

STOP IT!

I CAN'T STAND LISTENING TO THIS! I GIVE UP. YOU GUYS ARE HOPELESS!

WE TRIUMPH AGAIN.

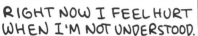

LIFE IN HELL

©1994 BY MATT GROENING

THE JOY OF CARTOON FAME

YOU DO THE SIMPSONS? WOW!

I HATE THE SIMPSONS!

COULD YOU DRAW ME A PICTURE OF SNOOPY?

I HAPPEN TO HAVE A COPY OF MISERY FOR YOU TO SIGN, MR. KING.

WHAT'S THE DEAL WITH AKBAR AND JEFF?! ARE THEY "WEIRD," OR WHAT?

WANNA TRADE ORIGINAL ART, MAN?

WOULD YOU MIND DRAWING ME A PICTURE OF MARGE SIMPSON NAKED? I WON'T SELL IT. IT'S FOR MY PRIVATE COLLECTION.

I JUST LOVED "DRACULA," MR. COPPOLA.

WOW! IT MUST BE **WILD** BEING MARRIED TO LYNDA BARRY.

IT IS, MAN.

WE REALLY DIDN'T APPRECIATE YOUR CARTOON STRIP THAT INSULTED PIERCING.

YOU GOTTA DRAW ME A PICTURE OF BART ON A HARLEY, HOLDING UP THE SEVERED HEAD OF MY GIRLFRIEND. SHE'LL LOVE IT!

I'M YOUR BIGGEST FAN IN THE WORLD. I'VE GOT ALL THE SIMPSONS COLLECTORS' PLATES.

THANKS A LOT.

"THANKS A LOT"? **THAT'S THE BEST YOU CAN DO??!**

COME **ON**, MAN. ALL WE NEED IS $48,000 OR THE PIGS ARE GONNA KICK US OUT OF OUR COMMUNE.

LOOK AT MY TATTOO, MAN! I'M YOUR BIGGEST FAN!

WOW!

MISSPELLED

BLINKY

WOULD YOU MIND IF I JUST FOLLOWED YOU AROUND FOR A LITTLE WHILE?

I GUESS I'D LIKE YOUR AUTOGRAPH, EVEN THOUGH YOU SOLD OUT TO HOLLYWOOD.

HEY, **LOOK EVERYBODY!!** HE'S DOIN' **FREE** SIMPSONS DRAWINGS!!

LIFE IN HELL

©1993 BY MATT GROENING

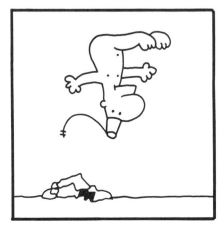

© 1989 BY MATT GROENING

LIFE IN HELL

©1993 BY MATT GROENING

©1993
BY MATT
GROENING

IF YOU THINK I'M GOING TO RESPOND TO YOUR HEAD EXPLODING, YOU'VE GOT ANOTHER THINK COMING.

GO AHEAD AND SULK.

YOU CAN'T LAY YOUR GUILT TRIP ON ME, MAN.

I'M NOT TROUBLED BY THIS AT ALL.

BTOOM!

I KNEW YOU CARED

©1993
BY MATT
GROENING

© 1992 BY MATT GROENING WITH JAMIE ANGELL

WON'T **YOU** HELP US PROFIT FROM THE RAGE AND MISERY OF OTHERS?

CALLING ALL SLOBS!

HIPPER THAN BOOTLEG BART SIMPSON T-SHIRTS!

Akbar & Jeff's Official L.A. Riots Souvenir T-Shirts

"BRINGING YOU THE FINEST IN EXPLOITATIVE FUNWEAR SINCE 1992"

I SURVIVED THE L.A. RIOTS TV NEWSCASTS

MY OTHER CAR IS ON FIRE

I BENEFITED FROM THE LIBERAL SOCIAL PROGRAMS OF THE SIXTIES AND ALL I GOT WAS THIS LOUSY T-SHIRT

I USED TO ♥ L.A.

RIOTERS DO IT IN A FRENZY

I'D RATHER BE LOOTING

MY POLITICAL LEADERS STARTED THE HEALING PROCESS AND ALL I GOT WAS THIS LOUSY T-SHIRT

THANK YOU FOR NOT KILLING ME

LIFE IN HELL

©1989 BY MATT GROENING

HOW TO STOP A THROBBING HEADACHE

NO ONE KNOWS EXACTLY WHAT CAUSES THEM. ONE MINUTE YOU'RE ALL PEACEFUL AND HAPPY, THE NEXT YOU FEEL LIKE HORNETS ARE FLYING AROUND INSIDE YOUR BRAIN -- FOR NO EXPLICABLE REASON.

HONEY-- I CAN'T FIND THE REMOTE CONTROL

QUICKLY, BEFORE IT GETS ANY WORSE, YOU MUST FIND A QUIET ROOM. LOCK THE DOOR, PULL THE SHADES, UNPLUG THE PHONE, TURN OFF THE LIGHTS, AND GET COMFORTABLE.

WHERE IS THAT REMOTE CONTROL?

TURN YOUR THOUGHTS INWARD. IGNORE ALL OUTSIDE STIMULI.

HONEY, ARE YOU IN THERE? THE DOOR IS LOCKED. BY ANY CHANCE DO YOU HAVE THE REMOTE CONTROL?

NOW BEGIN TO VISUALIZE YOUR PAIN. STAY WITH YOUR PAINFUL BRAIN IMAGE FOR SIXTY SECONDS.

WHO STOLE MY REMOTE CONTROL?

THEN, VERY SLOWLY, BEGIN TO IMAGINE YOUR HEADACHE CHANGING INTO SOMETHING MILDLY PLEASANT, IF NOT DOWNRIGHT AMUSING.

HELP!! QUICKSAND!!!

TRY TO IGNORE YOUR PAIN DURING THIS STEP. TAKE IT NICE AND EASY. ENJOY THE HEALING PROCESS.

I'LL NEVER ASK WHERE THE REMOTE CONTROL IS AGAIN!!

PRESTO! YOUR THROBBING HEADACHE IS GONE! WASN'T THAT SIMPLE?

NOW RETURN TO THE REAL WORLD, HAPPY AND REFRESHED.

OH, HONEY....

BUSH VETOES ABORTION AID FOR RAPE AND INCEST VICTIMS

©1992 BY MATT GROENING

WHAT COULD BE MORE SOPHISTICATED THAN A FASHION STATEMENT YOU CAN'T GET RID OF?

CALLING ALL COOL KIDS!
GET YOUR ALIENATED BUTTS DOWN TO

IT'S AS EASY AND CREATIVE AS PICKING OUT A GREETING CARD!

Akbar & Jeff's Tattoo Hut

"WHERE A PASSING FANCY CAN FOLLOW YOU TO YOUR GRAVE"

HERE JUST FOUR OF OUR CURRENT FAVORITES!

10% OFF FOR ANY MISSPELLINGS!

AS SEEN ON MTV AND "AMERICA'S MOST WANTED"

HEY MOM AND DAD! LOOK WHAT I SPENT MY DORM MONEY ON!

ASK ME ABOUT MY CASTRATION ANXIETY

COMMON QUESTIONS ABOUT TATTOOS

Q: DOES IT HURT TO GET TATTOOED?
A: NO MORE THAN A THOUSAND TINY FISHHOOKS BRIEFLY PRICKING YOU IN SUCCESSION.

Q: WHAT IF I GET MY TRUE LOVE'S NAME TATTOOED ON MY BODY AND WE BREAK UP?
A: THAT JUST IS NOT POSSIBLE.

OUR GUARANTEE

"YOU PROBABLY WON'T FEEL LIKE A JERK IN 10 YEARS JUST BECAUSE YOU HAVE A HEAVY METAL BAND'S LOGO ON YOUR BUTT"

ASK ABOUT OUR SPECIAL DESIGNS FOR MENTALLY ILL PERFORMANCE ARTISTS!

CAN YOU FIND THE GENITAL WARTS HIDDEN IN THIS PICTURE?

BORN TO MAKE MINIMUM WAGE

IMPORTANT: YOU MUST BE AT LEAST 18 YEARS OLD, NOT TOO BRIGHT, HATE YOUR PARENTS, AND HAVE CASH IN HAND

REMEMBER! IT'S NOT SELF-MUTILATION IF WE HELP YOU DO IT!

©1993
By MATT
GROENING

©1993
BY MATT
GROENING

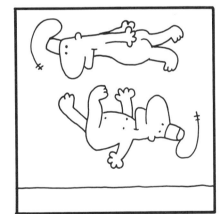

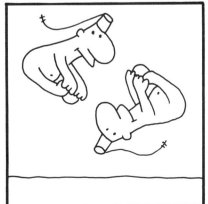

©1992 BY MATT GROENING

LIFE IN HELL

©1989 BY MATT GROENING

HOW TO GET BEYOND STRESS

Panel 1

LET'S FACE IT: WE ARE ALL STRESSED TO THE MAX. FOR SOME SENSITIVE PEOPLE, MERELY READING THE PHRASE "STRESSED TO THE MAX" CAUSES STRESS.

> I'M SO STRESSED I CAN BARELY STAND TO LOOK AT YOU.
> OOH, MOODY.

Panel 2

FEW OF US KNOW HOW TO GET BEYOND STRESS. WE YELL AT THE TV, WE HONK IN TRAFFIC, WE RIP UP OUR LOSING LOTTERY TICKETS, WE SNAP AT OUR LOVED ONES-- BUT SOMEHOW IT ISN'T ENOUGH.

> DON'T CALL ME MOODY, GRUMPY.
> DON'T CALL ME GRUMPY, MOODY.
> GRUMPY. MOODY.

Panel 3

SO WE TRY TO GET PEACE OF MIND BY EATING TASTY SNACK TREATS, PUFFING ON SOOTHING CIGARETTES, DRINKING DELICIOUS ALCOHOLIC BEVERAGES, OR SMOKING RELAXING CRACK.

> THIS IS THE LIFE, EH?
> WUZZA BLMPHA MRMBL GLMPH

Panel 4

AND YET WE OFTEN END UP JUST AS STRESSED AS WHEN WE STARTED.

> I HATE MYSELF FOR LOVING YOU.
> WE ARE ALIKE IN MANY WAYS.

Panel 5

SO HERE'S WHAT YOU MUST DO. SIT ON A COMFY SOFA IN A DARK, WARM, QUIET ROOM. TURN OFF THE TV, OR AT LEAST KEEP THE VOLUME DOWN.

> PLEASE DON'T WHISTLE.

Panel 6

STARE AT A BLANK WALL. BREATHE SLOWLY AND DEEPLY. EACH TIME YOU EXHALE, REPEAT THE WORD "STRESS" TO YOURSELF. THIS WILL BE YOUR MANTRA.

> STRESS STRESS STRESS STRESS STRESS STRESS STRESS STRESS STRESS STRESS STRESS

Panel 7

VISUALIZE YOUR BODY AS THE RUSTY, HOLLOW HULL OF A SUNKEN OCEAN FREIGHTER, AND THE WORD "STRESS" AS A GIANT EEL SWIMMING IN AND OUT OF YOUR PORTHOLES.

Panel 8

CONTINUE BREATHING DEEPLY WHILE THE EEL SLITHERS THROUGH YOUR DEPTHS. SOON THE EEL WILL SWIM AWAY, AND YOU WILL FEEL RELAXED AND REFRESHED.

> DON'T CALL ME PERKY, CHUCKLES.
> DON'T CALL ME CHUCKLES, PERKY.
> CHUCKLES. PERKY.

Panel 9

JUST LOOK AT ALL THE POOR SUCKERS AROUND YOU WHO ARE LIVING IN CONSTANT MENTAL TURMOIL. BUT NOT YOU! YOU HAVE ACHIEVED INNER PEACE. YOU SHOULD BE VERY PLEASED WITH YOURSELF.

> GRUMPY.
> MOODY.
> I FORGIVE YOU.

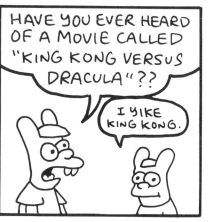

LIFE IN HELL

©1992 By Matt Groening

BEDTIME STORY

BY WILL GROENING AND HIS DAD

BUT I NOT SLEEPY.

TELL ME A STORY, DADDY LION.

OK, BABY LION.

ONCE UPON A TIME THERE WAS A PUPPY DOG.

AND HIS NAME WAS GROVER. AND GROVER THE PUPPY DOG WENT IN THE BACK YARD AND HE SAW...

A MONSTER!

AND GROVER RUN AWAY INTO THE FOREST AND CLIMB A TREE BECAUSE THE MONSTER WAS CHASING HIM WITH HIS TERRIBLE TEETH AND HIS TERRIBLE CLAWS.

THEN HE JUMP FROM THE TREE ONTO THE ROOF OF A HOUSE.

AND THERE WAS A GHOST!

SO THE PUPPY DOG RUN INSIDE AND THERE WAS A WITCH!

SO HE RUN IN THE BEDROOM AND THERE WAS A WOLF!

AND GROVER HIDE IN THE TOY CHEST!

THEN MOTHRA CAME.

MOTHRA?

MOTHRA THE GIANT CATERPILLAR.

AND HE CRUSH THE GAS STATION.

AND HE CRAWL IN THE CITY AND KNOCK DOWN THE BUILDINGS.

THEN MOTHRA MAKE A COCOON!

THEN WHAT HAPPENED?

MOTHRA COME OUT OF THE COCOON!

YOU KNOW SOMETHING? MOTHRA TURN INTO A BEAUTIFUL BUTTERFLY.

AND HE FLY AWAY.

I SLEEPING NOW. GO TO YOUR ROOM, DADDY LION.

IT'S PAINTASTIC!

IT'S DISFIGURE-IFFIC!

HEY KIDS!

YOU'VE TRIED THE REST-- NOW TRY RITUALISTIC BODY MUTILATION!!

Akbar & Jeff's Piercing Hut

SPECIALIZING IN EARS·EYEBROWS·LIPS· NOSES·TONGUES·AND MORE!

"WHERE YESTERDAY'S PSYCHOPATHOLOGY BECOMES TODAY'S MIDDLE-CLASS YOUTH-CULTURE AFFECTATION"

NOW YOU CAN WEAR YOUR ABUSED CHILDHOOD LIKE A BADGE!

AS SEEN ON MTV AND IN YOUR NIGHTMARES

WHAT'RE YOU LOOKIN' AT?

WHAT IS PIERCING?

PIERCING IS THE ACT OF PERFORATING, PUNCTURING, LANCING, OR CUTTING THROUGH THE BODY PART OF YOUR CHOICE FOR THE PURPOSE OF DANGLING A RING, BOLT, FISHING WEIGHT, OR OTHER METALLIC FETISH OBJECT AND THEREBY MAKING YOURSELF MORE BEAUTIFUL.

YES, WE CAN PIERCE YOUR PRIVATES!!!

IT'S FUN, CHIC, AND ALMOST SEMI-PAINLESS!

WARNING!

WE CANNOT BE HELD RESPONSIBLE FOR INJURIES INCURRED WHILE:

☆ HORSEBACK-RIDING
☆ MOUNTAIN-BIKING
☆ PLAYGROUND SEESAW-STRADDLING

YOU MUST BE AT LEAST 18 YEARS OLD, NOT EXACTLY BRIGHT, SEXUALLY ALIENATED, TORMENTED BY UNCONSCIOUS GUILT FEELINGS, RECONCILED TO DIMINISHED EMPLOYMENT OPPORTUNITIES, HAVE LITTLE OR NO SENSE OF THE FUTURE, AND BRING CASH IN HAND

REMEMBER! IT'S NOT SELF-MUTILATION IF WE HELP YOU DO IT!

LIFE IN HELL

© 1993 By Matt Groening

THE BALLAD OF AKBAR & JEFF

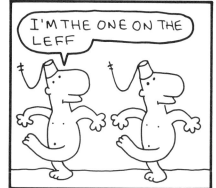

© 1994
BY MATT
GROENING

Panel 1: HEY, WILL — I'M UP AGAINST A DEADLINE AND I NEED YOUR HELP WITH MY COMIC STRIP.
AGAIN, DADDY?

Panel 2: OK. I WRITE THE WORDS AND YOU DRAW THE PICTURES, RIGHT, DADDY?
YEAH. IT'S CALLED COLLABORATION.

Panel 3: WHAAT?!!

Panel 4:
THE LEGEND OF GOD
BY WILL

WITH COMMENTARY BY ABE

Panel 5: AN OLD INDIAN CHIEF DECIDED TO PUT GOD TO THE EARTH SO HE SENT GOD TO EARTH.

Panel 6: THEN THE OLD INDIAN CHIEF SHOT BOW AND ARROWS INTO A TREE AND GOD APPEARED.

Panel 7: WHEN ALL THE PEOPLE DIED GOD TALKED TO THEM, BUT THEN GOD DIDN'T KNOW SOME THINGS.

Panel 8: HE TOLD THEM THAT THEIR BODY DIES BUT THEIR SPIRIT LIVES ON.

Panel 9: SOME PEOPLE THINK THAT DYING IS FUN.

Panel 10: I THINK DYING IS FUN.

Panel 11: DYING IS **NOT** FUN, ABE. WHEN YOU DIE THEY PUT YOU UNDER THE GROUND AND YOUR EYES ARE CLOSED.
NOT ME. I CAN FLY.

Panel 12: YOU CAN'T FLY! YOU HAVE TO STAY FOREVER AND EVER IN A LITTLE CAVE!
CAVES ARE TOO SCARY.

Panel 13: ACTUALLY, WE ALL USED TO BE CAVEMEN. WE HAD TO LIVE IN A CAVE ALL THE TIME! EVEN YOU, ABE!

Panel 14: I PLAY WITH MY TOYS IN THE CAVE.

Panel 15: CAVEMEN DIDN'T HAVE TOYS. CAVEMEN DIDN'T HAVE NOTHING. ALL THEY HAD WAS **CLUBS.**

Panel 16: NOT ME. I'M A TOY BOY.

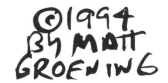
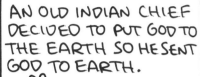

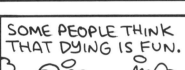

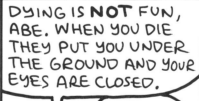

©1994 BY MATT GROENING

YOUR FLU CHECKLIST

- [ ] NAIVE OPTIMISM
- [ ] WHISTLING A JAUNTY TUNE
- [ ] WATCHING CO-WORKERS DROP LIKE FLIES
- [ ] GOBBLING FISTSFUL OF VITAMIN C
- [ ] "FUNNY" FEELING
- [ ] UH OH
- [ ] WANTING TO STRANGLE GUY WHO SAYS, "IS YOUR NOGGIN THROBBIN'?"
- [ ] FEELING GREEN AROUND THE GILLS
- [ ] FEEBLE GOODBYES TO ANNOYED CO-WORKERS
- [ ] CRAWLING HOME IN HEAVY TRAFFIC
- [ ] CRAWLING INTO BED
- [ ] TOSSING AND TURNING
- [ ] NIGHTMARES OF LYING AWAKE IN BED, SUFFERING HORRIBLY
- [ ] ACUTE SNIFFLING
- [ ] SEVERE SNUFFLING
- [ ] EXCESSIVE SNORKING
- [ ] ACHING SKIN
- [ ] ACHING EYEBALLS
- [ ] ACHING EVERYTHING
- [ ] ELECTRIC BLANKET ON HIGH
- [ ] SHIVERING LIKE A MEXICAN HAIRLESS
- [ ] ONE FOOT IN THE GRAVE

- [ ] PHLEGM MANIA!
- [ ] SHUFFLING DOWN THE HALL IN RATTY BATHROBE LIKE CRANKY OLD GEEZER
- [ ] CALLING DOCTOR AND BEING PUT ON HOLD FOR 45 MINUTES
- [ ] STANDING IN LINE WITH FRIGHTENING LOSERS AT PHARMACY
- [ ] REALIZING YOU'RE JUST AS FRIGHTENING
- [ ] GULPING WORTHLESS COLD-AND-FLU SYRUP
- [ ] DOWNING WORTHLESS ANTIBIOTICS
- [ ] SUCKING ON VILE LOZENGES
- [ ] THROWING USED KLEENEX AT WASTEBASKET AND MISSING
- [ ] SLURPING LOUSY DELICATESSEN CHICKEN SOUP
- [ ] PARANOID SUSPICION THAT YOU'RE IN A SECRET GOVERNMENT RADIATION EXPERIMENT
- [ ] HATRED OF WORLD
- [ ] FEELING A TAD BETTER, ONLY 10 YEARS OLDER
- [ ] WOBBLING BACK TO WORK
- [ ] SHARING EXTREMELY TEDIOUS SICKNESS STORIES
- [ ] GENTLE SNORKING
- [ ] WHISTLING A JAUNTY TUNE
- [ ] NAIVE OPTIMISM
- [ ] RELAPSE

LIFE IN HELL
10th ANNIVERSARY STRIP

©1990
BY MATT
GROENING

QUIET, PLEASE.

OUR TESTS SHOW YOU'RE NOT TRYING.

I WISH I COULD PASS YOU, BUT I JUST CAN'T.

THE COMPUTER SHOWS NO RECORD OF YOUR PAYMENT.

I'M SORRY, BUT WE CAN'T HELP YOU IF YOU DON'T HAVE YOUR RECEIPT.

I'M SORRY, BUT THAT'S NOT OUR POLICY.

I'M SORRY, BUT YOUR NAME ISN'T ON THE LIST.

I LOVE YOU, BUT I'M NOT IN LOVE WITH YOU.

MY, YOU LOOK TIRED.

PLEASE TRY TO SEE IT FROM THE COMPANY'S POINT OF VIEW.

CONGRATULATIONS ON YOUR HONORABLE MENTION.

PLEASE HOLD.

YOU'RE NOT GETTING ANY YOUNGER, YOU KNOW.

BUT FIRST, THESE IMPORTANT MESSAGES.

THANK YOU SO MUCH FOR ALL YOUR COOPERATION.

LIFE IN HELL

© 1989 BY MATT GROENING

BINKY'S SEARCH FOR ENLIGHTENMENT

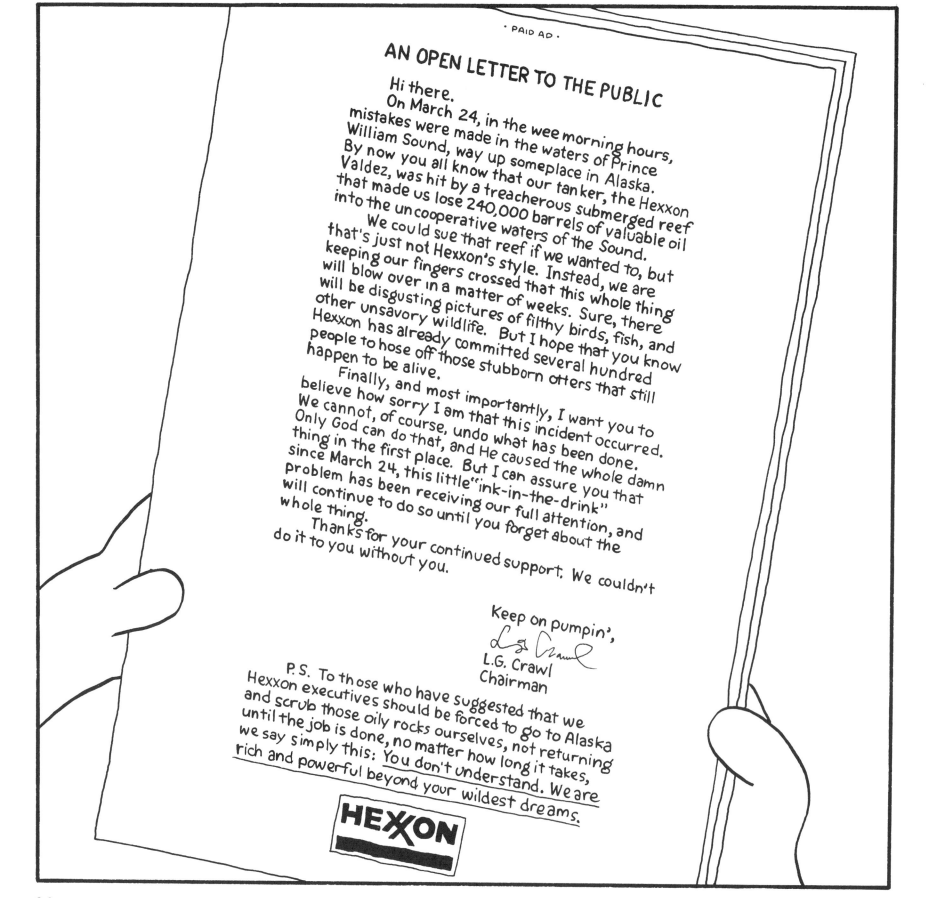

· PAID AD ·

AN OPEN LETTER TO THE PUBLIC

Hi there.

On March 24, in the wee morning hours, mistakes were made in the waters of Prince William Sound, way up someplace in Alaska. By now you all know that our tanker, the Hexxon Valdez, was hit by a treacherous submerged reef that made us lose 240,000 barrels of valuable oil into the uncooperative waters of the Sound.

We could sue that reef if we wanted to, but that's just not Hexxon's style. Instead, we are keeping our fingers crossed that this whole thing will blow over in a matter of weeks. Sure, there will be disgusting pictures of filthy birds, fish, and other unsavory wildlife. But I hope that you know Hexxon has already committed several hundred people to hose off those stubborn otters that still happen to be alive.

Finally, and most importantly, I want you to believe how sorry I am that this incident occurred. We cannot, of course, undo what has been done. Only God can do that, and He caused the whole damn thing in the first place. But I can assure you that since March 24, this little "ink-in-the-drink" problem has been receiving our full attention, and will continue to do so until you forget about the whole thing.

Thanks for your continued support. We couldn't do it to you without you.

Keep on pumpin',

L.G. Crawl
Chairman

P.S. To those who have suggested that we Hexxon executives should be forced to go to Alaska and scrub those oily rocks ourselves, not returning until the job is done, no matter how long it takes, we say simply this: You don't understand. We are rich and powerful beyond your wildest dreams.

HEXXON

LIFE IN HELL

© 1993 BY MATT GROENING

I'M SORRY ABOUT LAST NIGHT.

FORGET ABOUT IT.

TO WAKE YOU UP FROM A DEEP SLEEP AT 2 AM BY SCREECHING IN YOUR FACE WAS QUITE AWFUL OF ME.

THAT'S WATER UNDER THE BRIDGE.

I SHOULDN'T HAVE CALLED YOU ALL THOSE VILE, VICIOUS NAMES.

WELL, IT'S OVER AND DONE WITH.

I CAN'T BELIEVE I HEAVED THAT VCR AT YOU WITH SUCH ACCURACY.

THAT'S THE PAST.

AND WHEN THE NEIGHBORS CALLED THE POLICE, I WAS MORTIFIED.

DON'T WORRY ABOUT IT.

WHY THE COPS PICKED YOU TO BEAT UP INSTEAD OF ME IS A REAL MYSTERY.

THESE THINGS HAPPEN.

I'M ASHAMED TO ADMIT I WAS CHUCKLING WHEN THEY HOGTIED YOU AND HAULED YOU OFF TO THE SLAMMER.

HEY, THAT'S LIFE.

THEN YOU FORGIVE ME?

YOU'LL HAVE TO WAIT TILL 2 AM FOR MY ANSWER.

© 1993 BY MATT GROENING

LIFE IN HELL

©1993 BY MATT GROENING

MY THERAPIST SAYS MAINTAINING A RELATIONSHIP IS HARD WORK.

MY THERAPIST SAYS EVERYTHING IS YOUR FAULT.

MY THERAPIST SAYS WE SHOULDN'T DUMP OUR FRUSTRATIONS ON EACH OTHER.

MY THERAPIST SAYS I CAN DO BETTER THAN HANGING OUT WITH A LOSER LIKE YOU.

MY THERAPIST SAYS WE NEED TO VALUE EACH OTHER'S DESIRES AS HIGHLY AS WE VALUE OUR OWN.

MY THERAPIST SAYS IF IT WEREN'T FOR YOU, EVERYTHING WOULD BE JUST FINE.

MY THERAPIST SAYS WE MUST LEARN TO HAVE EMPATHY FOR EACH OTHER.

MY THERAPIST SAYS YOU'VE GOT TO LEARN TO KEEP YOUR BIG MOUTH SHUT.

MY THERAPIST SAYS WE'VE GOT TO LEARN TO MANAGE OUR ANGER MORE EFFECTIVELY.

MY THERAPIST SAYS I'M FULLY JUSTIFIED IN SMASHING YOUR FACE IN.

MY THERAPIST SAYS WE HAVE TO LEARN CONFLICT RESOLUTION.

MY THERAPIST SAYS YOU'RE A SICK AND TWISTED INDIVIDUAL.

MY THERAPIST SAYS WE HAVE TO LEARN TO COMMUNICATE OUR NEEDS AND VULNERABILITIES.

MY THERAPIST SAYS YOU SOUND LIKE A REAL JERK.

I THINK I NEED TO GET A BETTER THERAPIST.

©1993 BY MATT GROENING

©1993
By Matt
Groening

LIFE IN HELL

© 1992 BY MATT GROENING

A BRIEF HISTORY OF MY LOUSY MOOD

1968 BEFORE

PLEASE DON'T LET THE RIGHT-WING SLEAZEBALL WIN.

AFTER

1972 BEFORE

PLEASE DON'T LET THE RIGHT-WING SLEAZEBALL WIN AGAIN.

AFTER

1976 BEFORE

PLEASE DON'T LET THE RIGHT-WING SLEAZEBALL WIN.

AFTER

YAY.

1980 BEFORE

PLEASE DON'T LET THE RIGHT-WING SLEAZEBALL WIN.

AFTER

1984 BEFORE

PLEASE DON'T LET THE RIGHT-WING SLEAZEBALL WIN AGAIN.

AFTER

1988 BEFORE

PLEASE DON'T LET THE RIGHT-WING SLEAZEBALL WIN.

AFTER

1992 BEFORE

PLEASE DON'T LET THE RIGHT-WING SLEAZEBALL WIN AGAIN.

AFTER

CHOOSE ONE.

YAY.

©1993 BY MATT GROENING

LIFE IN HELL

© 1993 BY MATT GROENING

SO HOW WAS SCHOOL TODAY?

LOOK, MAN, MY CLASSROOM IS PACKED TO THE GILLS WITH CONFUSED, NEGLECTED KIDS.

BECAUSE OF BUDGET CUTBACKS, THE SCHOOL LIBRARY IS CLOSED, WHICH NOBODY NOTICES BECAUSE NOBODY READS.

THE SCHOOL BUILDING IS FALLING APART, WE'VE GOT NO ART SUPPLIES, THERE'S A CHALK SHORTAGE, AND THE ONE OUTDATED COMPUTER IS BROKEN.

THE TEACHERS ARE STRESSED OUT BECAUSE OF THE LONG HOURS, THE OVERCROWDING, AND THE LATEST PAY CUTS.

THE KIDS ALTERNATE BETWEEN GIDDINESS AND STUPEFACTION, WAITING FOR THE BELL TO RING.

WE HAVE NO SENSE OF LOGIC, NO HISTORICAL AWARENESS, NO ANALYTICAL SKILLS, NO COMMAND OF LANGUAGE, AND THE ATTENTION SPAN OF A GNAT.

SO I'M THINKING OF DROPPING OUT.

BUT WITHOUT A GOOD EDUCATION, YOUR LIFE WILL GO NOWHERE.

©1992 BY MATT GROENING

CALLING ALL CARNAL CONSUMERS!
YOU'VE SEEN HER BREASTS -- NOW SEE THE BEST!

GRIM AND JOYLESS PSEUDO-SADOMASOCHISM --
THE KIND AMERICA LIKES!

LIFE IN HELL

©1993 BY MATT GROENING

© 1993 BY MATT GROENING

We're bombing Iraq again.

Yeah, but a lot of the bombs are missing their targets.

Yeah, but that means more innocent people could get killed.

Yeah, but we'll never really know.

Yeah, but that's no excuse for complacency.

Yeah, but what are you going to do when your own government lies to you?

Yeah, but are we just going to allow ourselves to be confused?

Yeah, but how can we know what we're confused about when we're so numb to everything?

Yeah, but at least we have the satisfaction of knowing we got rid of Bush.

Yeah, but Clinton says he supports Bush all the way.

Yeah, but just because it sounds like business as usual doesn't mean it's business as usual.

Yeah, but maybe we got fooled once again.

Yeah, but the inauguration is going to be so exciting.

Yeah, but weren't we talking about something important a few seconds ago?

Yeah, but there's a "yeah, but" for everything.

Yeah, but look at those celebrities boogie!

©1993 BY MATT GROENING

©1993 By Matt Groening

WHAT WILL YOU DO IF I DIE BEFORE YOU?

I'LL DANCE ON YOUR GRAVE.

I'LL SPIT ON YOUR GRAVE.

I'LL DIG UP YOUR BODY AND SELL YOUR ORGANS TO A THIRD-RATE MEDICAL SCHOOL.

I'LL DIG UP YOUR BODY AND SELL YOUR ORGANS TO A CREEPY NEW YORK PERFORMANCE ARTIST.

I'LL DIG UP YOUR SKELETON AND FEED YOUR BONES TO STREET DOGS.

I'LL SPRAYPAINT POLKA DOTS ON YOUR TOMBSTONE.

I'LL KEEP SHOUTING "SO LONG, SUCKER" AT YOUR FUNERAL.

I'LL SCATTER YOUR CREMATED ASHES IN A DEPRESSING LOS ANGELES MINI-MALL PARKING LOT.

I'LL HAVE YOU BURIED IN THE HAMSTER SECTION OF A PET CEMETERY.

I'LL BRIBE THE EMBALMER TO MAKE YOU LOOK EXTRA-PUFFY.

I'LL FILL YOUR COFFIN WITH ANNOYING STYROFOAM PACKING PELLETS.

I'LL HAVE YOU BURIED IN THAT ITCHY WOOL SWEATER YOU HATE.

LET'S QUIT THIS HOSTILE BANTER. I'M TIRED OF THINKING ABOUT YOUR DEATH.

YOU DON'T LOVE ME ANYMORE.

©1993 BY MATT GROENING

AKBAR & JEFF'S LIBRARY

WOULD YOU MIND CHEWING YOUR PEANUT BRITTLE A LITTLE MORE QUIETLY? I'M TRYING TO WATCH TV

BY AKBAR

OH SHUT UP

BY JEFF

NO, YOU SHUT UP

BY AKBAR

OH SHUT UP
VOLUME TWO

BY JEFF

BY THE WAY, DID I EVER MENTION HOW MUCH I HATE YOU?

BY AKBAR

SAME TO YOU AND MORE OF IT

BY JEFF

IF YOU THINK I'M GOING TO SIT HERE FOR THE REST OF MY LIFE AND PUT UP WITH YOUR ABUSE, YOU'RE CRAZY

BY AKBAR

YOU'RE THE ONE WHO'S CRAZY

BY JEFF

I HATE YOU YET I LOVE YOU

THE BEST OF AKBAR AND JEFF

LIFE IN HELL

©1993 BY MATT GROENING

WHY IS THE TV SAYING AMERICA IS PROUD AGAIN?

WE JUST BOMBED IRAQ AGAIN IN OUR WAR AGAINST TERRORISM.

DID WE WIN THE WAR AGAINST TERRORISM?

NOBODY KNOWS.

HOW MANY TERRORISTS DID WE KILL?

NOBODY KNOWS.

WE DIDN'T KILL TOO MANY INNOCENT PEOPLE, DID WE?

NOBODY KNOWS.

HOW MANY TERRORISTS DID WE KILL LAST TIME?

NOBODY KNOWS.

HOW MANY INNOCENT PEOPLE DID WE KILL LAST TIME?

NOBODY KNOWS.

I KNOW THIS IS OFF THE SUBJECT, BUT WHEN WILL DEMOCRACY BE ESTABLISHED IN KUWAIT?

NOBODY KNOWS.

HOW DO WE KNOW HOW PROUD WE SHOULD BE?

WE HAVE TO USE OUR IMAGINATIONS.

LIFE IN HELL

© 1993 BY MATT GROENING

I HAVE TO GO OUT FOR A LITTLE WHILE. IF YOU REALLY LOVE ME, YOU WON'T DO ANY SCAT-SINGING BEHIND MY BACK.

FINE. I ASK THE SAME OF YOU.

SKOODLY.

SKOODLY-DEE.

SKOODLY-DEE-DIDDLE-DEE-WAH.

DEE-DIDDLE-DEE DOODILY-DIDDLE-DEE-DOO.

DEE-SKIDDLY.

WIDDLY-WOO-YAH-WEE-WIDDLY-DIDDLY-DEE-DAH.

DEE-DOODLY-DEE-DOOP-DEE-DOO.

SKEEBA-SKOOBA-DEE-SKEEBA-DEE-SKOO.

BE-BOP-A-DOODLE-UM-BE-BOP-A-DOO.

I BELIEVE YOU BETRAYED MY TRUST.

YOU'RE A SICK, SUSPICIOUS LITTLE INDIVIDUAL. I DON'T DISTRUST **YOU**.

I'M SORRY.

SKOODLY-OODLY-DOODLY DOO.

©1994 BY MATT GROENING

© 1994 BY MATT GROENING

©1993 By MATT GROENING

©1993
By MATT GROENING
THANKS TO MARK GATEWOOD

LIFE IN HELL

©1994 BY MATT GROENING

ALL MY LIFE I'VE HAD A TROUBLED HEART.

I'VE BEEN TORMENTED BY THE PERVASIVENESS OF SUFFERING IN THE WORLD.

I'VE BEEN PERTURBED BY LIFE'S INEVITABLE LOSSES.

I'VE BEEN THOROUGHLY FREAKED OUT BY MY OWN AGING AND IMPENDING DEATH.

HOW I'VE LONGED FOR SOME RELIEF FROM THE PAIN I FEEL.

I'VE IMMERSED MYSELF IN PHILOSOPHY, BUT SADLY, THAT HAS BEEN ULTIMATELY UNSATISFYING.

I'VE ENGAGED IN DEEP MEDITATION, BUT THE INSIGHTS I'VE GAINED HAVE ONLY BEEN PARTIALLY CONSOLING.

I'VE STUDIED THE GREAT SPIRITUAL TEACHERS OF THE WORLD, BUT STILL I NEED MORE.

I'VE SOUGHT AWARENESS IN PSYCHOANALYSIS, BUT AFTER SEVERAL YEARS ON THE COUCH, I FEEL ONLY A LITTLE CLOSER TO THE TRUTH.

I'VE EVEN SOUGHT LIBERATION IN CARNAL DESIRE, BUT ALAS-- THOSE MOMENTS OF RAPTURE HAVE BEEN ALL TOO FLEETING.

BUT TODAY, AFTER ALL THESE YEARS OF SEARCHING.... SOMETHING AMAZING HAPPENED.

I WAS OUT TAKING A WALK, WHEN SUDDENLY A SMALL, SHINY PEBBLE CAUGHT MY EYE.

AS I GAZED INTO THE SMOOTH TEXTURE OF THIS TINY PEBBLE THAT I HELD IN THE PALM OF MY HAND, EVERYTHING BECAME CLEAR, AND I WAS COSMICALLY UNITED WITH THE UNIVERSE.

FOR THE FIRST TIME IN MY LONG SPIRITUAL JOURNEY, I FEEL TRUE PEACE.

I PUT SOME PROZAC IN YOUR CORNFLAKES THIS MORNING.

©1992 BY MATT GROENING

ARE YOU TOTALLY FED UP WITH THE STUPID, HATEFUL, ABUSIVE, INSENSITIVE, PSYCHOTIC, LYING, DISGUSTING JERK YOU LIVE WITH, AND WOULD YOU LIKE TO WORK THINGS OUT? THEN GET YOUR WOUNDED INNER CHILD DOWN TO

Akbar & Jeff's COUPLES THERAPY CENTER

"WHERE THE ELITE MEET TO BERATE"

THERAPIST AKBAR

WOULD YOU PLEASE SHUT YOUR BIG FAT MOUTH WHEN I'M MAKING A DIAGNOSIS?

CAN'T WE PLEASE BE PROFESSIONAL, "TINY"? AND I DO MEAN "TINY."

REFEREE JEFF

TRY OUR SPECIAL 4-PART HEALING PROCESS!

WARM-UP EXERCISES

COMPLETE THIS SENTENCE: "IF MY PARTNER WERE A FARM ANIMAL, HE WOULD NO DOUBT BE ____." A SMELLY, PASSIVE-AGGRESSIVE MULE, FOR INSTANCE.

UNCOVERING YOUR HIDDEN HURTS

YOU MUST PREFACE YOUR REMARKS WITH THE PHRASE "I HONESTLY FEEL." TRY IT THIS WAY: "I HONESTLY FEEL IF YOU DON'T GET OFF MY CASE I WILL BASH YOUR HEAD IN WHILE YOU SLEEP."

RECEIVING BRUTAL INSIGHTS

THE REASON WE CHARGE SO MUCH IS BECAUSE YOU'RE A COUPLE OF INCREDIBLY BORING WHINERS.

CLOSURE

I'M SORRY TO CUT YOU OFF IN MID-SENTENCE, BUT OUR TIME IS UP FOR TODAY. PLEASE TRY TO WEEP QUIETLY ON YOUR WAY OUT.

FUN!

EDUCATIONAL!

"WE PUT THE FUN BACK IN DYSFUNCTIONAL!"

©1994 BY MATT GROENING

WHY DID THE U.S. GOVERNMENT CONDUCT SECRET RADIATION TESTS ON UNSUSPECTING TEENAGED BOYS?

WELL, DON'T GET HUFFY. IT WASN'T JUST TEENAGED BOYS.

THEY ALSO DID SECRET RADIATION EXPERIMENTS ON SOLDIERS, HOSPITAL PATIENTS, PRISONERS, AND OLD FOLKS.

NOT TO MENTION PREGNANT WOMEN.

BUT THE GOOD THING IS THOSE DAYS -- FROM THE 1940s TO THE 1970s -- ARE OVER.

NOW THAT WE'VE GOTTEN THESE DISTURBING REVELATIONS OUT OF THE WAY, WE CAN GET ON WITH OUR LIVES IN A SPIRIT OF HONESTY, OPENNESS, AND TRUST.

CARE FOR SOME MILK AND COOKIES?

YOU GO FIRST.

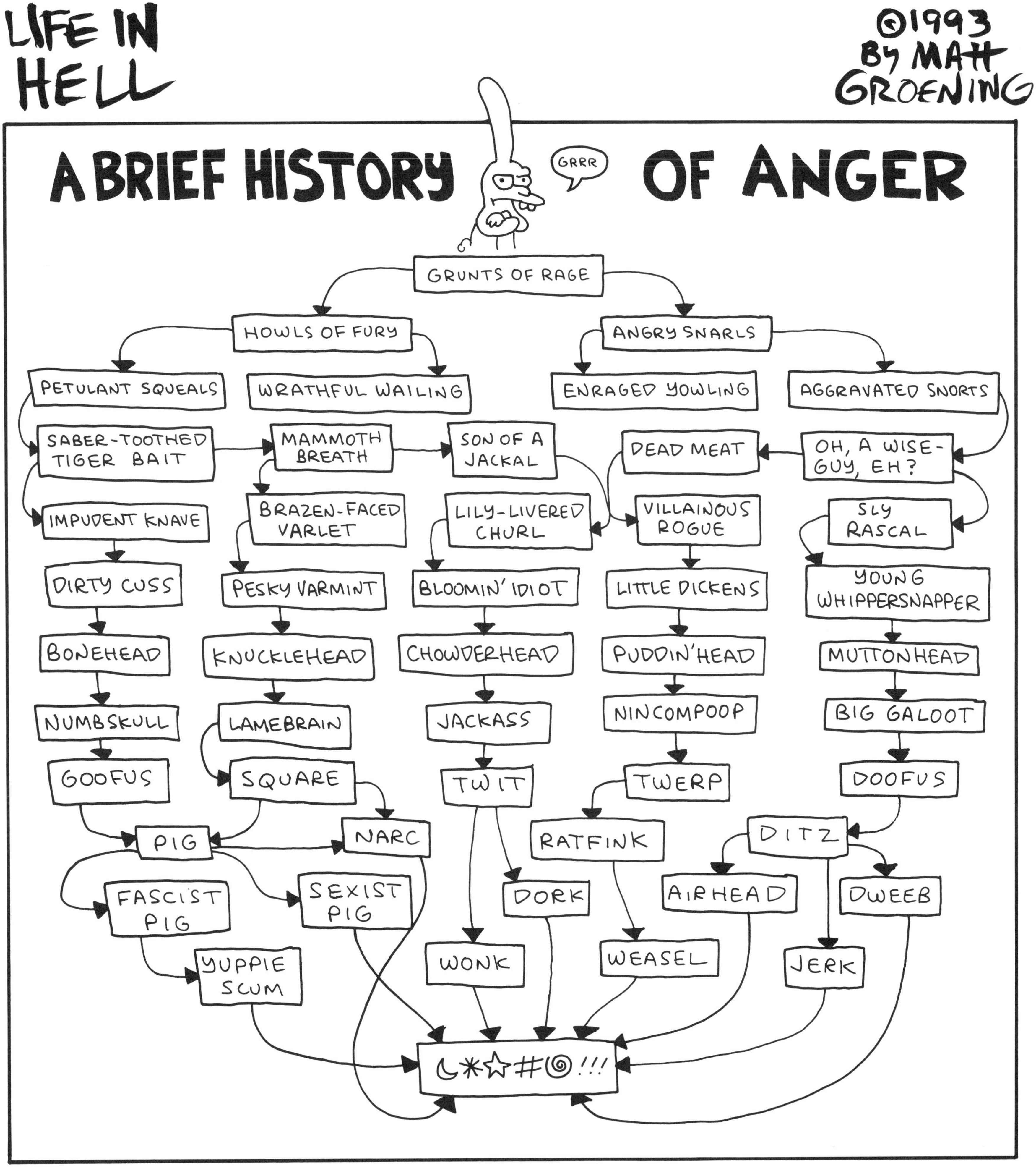
LIFE IN HELL
©1993 BY MATT GROENING
A BRIEF HISTORY OF ANGER
GRRR
GRUNTS OF RAGE
HOWLS OF FURY
ANGRY SNARLS
PETULANT SQUEALS
WRATHFUL WAILING
ENRAGED YOWLING
AGGRAVATED SNORTS
SABER-TOOTHED TIGER BAIT
MAMMOTH BREATH
SON OF A JACKAL
DEAD MEAT
OH, A WISE-GUY, EH?
IMPUDENT KNAVE
BRAZEN-FACED VARLET
LILY-LIVERED CHURL
VILLAINOUS ROGUE
SLY RASCAL
DIRTY CUSS
PESKY VARMINT
BLOOMIN' IDIOT
LITTLE DICKENS
YOUNG WHIPPERSNAPPER
BONEHEAD
KNUCKLEHEAD
CHOWDERHEAD
PUDDIN'HEAD
MUTTONHEAD
NUMBSKULL
LAMEBRAIN
JACKASS
NINCOMPOOP
BIG GALOOT
GOOFUS
SQUARE
TWIT
TWERP
DOOFUS
PIG
NARC
RATFINK
DITZ
FASCIST PIG
SEXIST PIG
DORK
AIRHEAD
DWEEB
YUPPIE SCUM
WONK
WEASEL
JERK
☾*☆#◎!!!

LIFE IN HELL

©1994 BY MATT GROENING

A PENNY FOR YOUR THOUGHTS.

I'M ADDICTED TO YOU.

AND YOU'RE PROUD OF THAT?

ADDICTION IS VERY, VERY BAD, YOU KNOW.

SURE, IT TEMPORARILY ERADICATES PAIN, BUT AT WHAT COST?

THE PLEASURE YOU FEEL IS A COMPLETE SHAM.

IT GIVES YOU AN ARTIFICIAL SENSE OF SELF-ESTEEM.

YOU MAY THINK YOU'RE FEELING INTIMACY, BUT YOU'RE JUST KIDDING YOURSELF.

WHATEVER SENSE OF CONTROL YOU FEEL IS UTTERLY BOGUS.

THINGS MAY SEEM WONDERFUL WHEN THEY'RE ACTUALLY HORRIBLE.

IT IS A SHALLOW SUBSTITUTE FOR FACING UP TO THE REAL PAIN OF LIFE.

YOU'LL NEVER KNOW HOW AWFUL THE TRUTH REALLY IS.

I'M COMPLETELY DEVASTATED BY YOUR WISDOM.

DO YOU THINK WE SHOULD BREAK UP?

AS LONG AS WE REALIZE HOW UNHAPPY WE REALLY ARE, WE CAN BE TOGETHER FOREVER.

© 1994 BY MATT GROENING

LIFE IN HELL

©1993 BY Matt GROENING

DO YOU LOVE ME?

WELL, WHAT'S THE OPPOSITE OF LOVE?

IS IT HATE?

OR COMPLETE INDIFFERENCE TO SOMEONE WE LOVED IN THE PAST?

OR SOMETHING CLOSE TO INDIFFERENCE, COMBINED WITH A LITTLE ANNOYANCE?

OR HOSTILITY, COMBINED WITH ENVY?

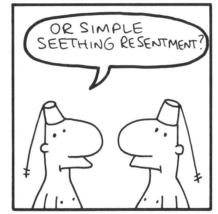

OR SIMPLE SEETHING RESENTMENT?

OR ACTIVE DESPISING MIXED WITH ANGER AND VENGEANCE?

WELL, I GUESS IT'S HATE.

BUT ISN'T HATE A FORM OF LOVE?

YOU MEAN, WHEREVER THERE IS HATE, LOVE MIGHT JUST BE AROUND THE CORNER?

MAYBE.

IN THAT CASE, I THINK I HATE YOU VERY MUCH.

AND I HATE YOU WITH ALL MY HEART.

STRANGELY, THIS COULD BE THE SWEETEST MOMENT WE'VE EVER HAD.

©1993
BY MATT
GROENING

LIFE IN HELL

©1994 BY MATT GROENING

YOU LIED TO ME.

YOU LIED TO ME ABOUT SANTA CLAUS.

YOU LIED TO ME ABOUT THE EASTER BUNNY.

YOU LIED TO ME ABOUT THE TOOTH FAIRY.

YOU LIED TO ME ABOUT GOD.

YOU LIED TO ME ABOUT WHAT HAPPENED TO MY PET HAMSTER.

YOU LIED TO ME ABOUT HISTORY.

YOU LIED TO ME ABOUT THE GOVERNMENT.

YOU LIED TO ME ABOUT MY BEDTIME.

YOU LIED TO ME ABOUT SEX.

YOU LIED TO ME ABOUT DRUGS.

YOU LIED TO ME ABOUT MY PROSPECTS IN LIFE.

YOU LIED TO ME ABOUT THAT DOG WHO WAS RIDING THAT OTHER DOG.

I'D LIKE TO SEE YOU COME UP WITH ONE BIG LIE TO EXPLAIN ALL YOUR OTHER LIES.

YOU MEAN **MY** PARENTS **LIED** TO ME?

©1993 BY MATT GROENING

©1993 BY MATT GROENING

DO YOU REALIZE THAT THE FOODS WE INGEST CAUSE STRESS AND SICKNESS?

OF COURSE. WHAT DO YOU THINK ALL THAT SUGAR, SALT, CAFFEINE, MEAT, OIL, AND FAT DOES? MAKES OUR COMPLEXIONS SPARKLE?

WE'RE PUTTING EXTREME STRESS ON OUR HEARTS, BRAINS, STOMACHS, AND OTHER VITAL ORGANS.

WHAT WE EAT DULLS OUR MINDS.

WE CLOG OUR ARTERIES EVERY DAY AT EVERY MEAL.

WE MAKE OURSELVES FAT AND LETHARGIC.

WE SLIP INTO A SLEEPY-EYED STUPOR.

OF THE TEN MAJOR CAUSES OF DEATH, NINE ARE LINKED TO WHAT WE EAT AND DRINK.

WITH EVERY BITE WE'RE BETRAYING OUR BODIES.

THE SAD PART IS IT'S ALL JUST COMPENSATION FOR FEELING UNLOVED.

WELL, DO YOU LOVE ME?

NOT REALLY.

DO YOU LOVE ME?

NOT REALLY.

ICE CREAM?

EXTRA SPRINKLES, PLEASE.

@1994 BY MATT GROENING

© 1994
By Matt
Groening

© 1994 BY MATT GROENING

STUDY QUESTIONS

by Professor Jamie Angell, Noted Rabbitologist

WARNING: These study questions are intended solely for the edification of you, the reader. Any unauthorized duplication of these questions will only mean you will have to answer them twice. Why bother?

AKBAR&JEFF

1. Akbar & Jeff each wear a fez. Sometimes they seem aroused by their fezzes. The word "fez" sounds a lot like "fizz." Also "fuzz." Also "floozy." Would you ever want to wear a fez? Don't be afraid to tell the truth.

2. Who do you like more: the simple, kind, gentle Akbar or the deceitful, cruel, malicious Jeff? This may be a trick question. Explain why you do, or do not, think this is so.

3. In the cartoon on page 43, what do you think Akbar is trying to make Jeff understand? What do you think the phrase "carnal delight" means to each of them? How do you interpret Jeff's remark "Sex is fun"? From this conversation what would you say is Akbar's dominant feeling toward Dan Quayle? Discuss.

4. When depicting a couple in bed, Groening usually draws the headboard to the right of the frame. When Akbar & Jeff are in bed, the headboard is to the left. Can this divergent recumbency be construed as:

    a) another sign, foretold in Revelations, of the impending Apocalypse?

    b) a secret message whose import is known only to the initiated?

    c) an irritating anomaly?

    d) all of the above?

5. Select a lettered pair that BEST expresses a relationship similar to that expressed in the original pair.

    AKBAR : JEFF ::

    a) pandemonium : bedlam

    b) wily : crafty

    c) frolicsome : frisky

    d) facsimile : duplicate

    e) Jeff : Akbar

RABBITS

1. Binky never seems to run out of wise sayings. Binky never seems to be truly happy. Which would you rather be, wise or happy? Have you ever been happy? Are you sure? What is happiness? Would you need to be wise to know you were happy? Express what you think and feel in a short, unhappy essay.

2. The cartoon on page 13 features a glass of love that Binky thinks is half empty and Sheba thinks is half full. What, in your opinion, is contained in this glass of love? Would you drink it? If it were boiled first, would you? Discuss.

3. Is it possible to ascertain the true extent of Binky's craving for chili on page 27 in light of his previous admission that he has a "tendency to lie"? Explain, supporting your opinion with citations from the text. Any inferences drawn from your own personal experience of the world will, naturally, be disallowed.

4. Suppose you were a talent scout looking for actors to make BINKY'S GUIDE TO LOVE into a movie. Briefly describe the kind of person you think each one should be. Give a general picture of the physical appearance of each, but focus major attention on overbites and hats. In conclusion, explain why you do, or do not, feel a top-notch makeup artist is crucial to recovering your investment in this project.

5. Select the lettered pair that BEST expresses a relationship similar to that expressed in the original pair.

BINKY : SHEBA ::

  a) repressed emotion : emotional repression
  b) angst : fahrvergnUgen
  c) Minneapolis : St. Paul
  d) Inky-bay : Eba-shay
  e) Tinker Toys : Leggos

GENERAL

1. What overall theme do you think is brought out through the reading of this book? Was it suggested or implied by one or more of the characters, or was it hammered mercilessly into your skull in a concerted and remorseless drumbeat of despair? Do you think the book has a specific purpose in addition to providing those involved with a financially rewarding experience? If so, what was the purpose?

2. If P(3,0) and Q (3,4) are two vertices of right triangle PQR, which of the following could NOT be the coordinates of R?

  a) (0,0)
  b) (0,4)
  c) (Akbar, Jeff)
  d) (Beaverton, OR)
  e) (Hell)

3. Choose one of the following quotations from the book that expresses an idea or opinion about which you have defi-

nite thoughts and feelings. Then write an essay in which you make clear what these thoughts and feeling are, doing your best to convey a familiarity with and knowledge of the book, which you, in fact, do not possess. Refer, if you like, to events in the book itself, or to something you have seen, a rumor you've heard, or a favorite joke. Or make something up. Go ahead. Lie. It doesn't matter. Our diagnostic

tests have already determined your place in society anyway.

  a) "Is love worth all the misery, or is all the misery worth all the misery?"
  b) "Ask me about my castration anxiety."
  c) "When you say you hate me it makes me think maybe you don't love me."
  d) "Abe is the baby walrus."

4. In a composition of several paragraphs, present the advantages and disadvantages of Groening's style of drawing. In your concluding paragraph, tell why you do, or do not, think this style is the result of:

  a) a thoroughly researched and carefully considered judgment
  b) the subconscious drift toward concept over craft in postmodern art
  c) market forces
  d) an inability to draw

5. The three basic elements of cartooning -- and real estate -- are location, location, location. To learn more about cartooning, answer the following three questions. Where did you get the money to buy this book? Where is the rest of your money? Where should we come to pick it up?

6. "Life in Hell" seemed like a funny title for a strip when it first came out. Does it still seem funny? Just what is so funny about it anyway? What makes you think it's so funny? You want to make something out of it?

Fold your answer sheet neatly, place it in a stamped, self-addressed envelope, seal the envelope, and mail it to yourself. Then put your feet up. Relax. Wait for the cash to roll in. Continue waiting. Have a nice life.

INDEX

A

AHOY, 31
AIRBRUSHED HAMBURGERS, 40
AIRPORT, 23, 56, 64
AKBAR & JEFF INC.:
    Beachside Souvenir 'n' Snack Hut, 38
    Couples Therapy Center, 109
    Library, 101
    Muffinatorium, 56
    Official L.A. Riots Souvenir T-shirts, 68
    Piercing Hut, 79
    SEX the book, 96
    Tattoo Hut, 71
    ALIENATION
    of butts, 71
    throughout life, 84
ANGER, personal warning signs of, 53
ANTS, metaphysical speculation about, 50

B

BABY
    shower, 22
    talk, 7, 11, 16, 12, 33, 54, 83
    walrus, 83
BAGPIPE MUSIC, 45
"BALLAD OF AKBAR & JEFF," 80
BARBIE DOLL, 25
BATMANIA HEADQUARTERS, 38
BEATLE VS. BEETLE, 91
BED, conversations in, 10, 11, 18, 20, 46

BEEF-A-RONI, 40
BEEF JERKY, 9
BELCH, 25
    odd gaseous, 45
BIBLE BUDDY, 27
BITTER
    coffee, 7
    loneliness, 17
    memories, 12
    rage, 8
    recriminations, 34
    soul, 8
    wallowing in bitterness, 15
BLIMP-NOSE, 9
BOOMERANG, 118
BOUNCE-BUNNIES, 52
BRA, 25, 37, 96
BRINY DEEP, 38
BROADWAY TUNES, 45, 56
BRONTOSAURUS, 45
BUBONIC PLAGUE, 45
BUCKET, of horrors, 37
BUMPER CARS, 7
"BUSH VETOES ABORTION AID FOR RAPE AND INCEST VICTIMS," 70
    SEE ALSO Sleazeball, right-wing
BUTTERSCOTCH PUDDING, 31

C

CADUCEUS, 71
CARNALITY
    consumers of, 96
    delight in, 43
    desire for, 12, 108
    tension of, 10
    wiles of, 37, 52
CASTRATION ANXIETY, 71

CAT(S)
    the betrayal of your loyal little, 9, 20
    declarations of love for, 56
    diet, 31
    murderous thoughts of, 50
    obsession with, 21, 22
    Picasso, 15
    transfiguration of, 83
CELEBRITIES BOOGIE, 98
CHAIRS, comfy folding, 56
CHALK, shortage of, 95
CHANNELS, the changing of, 9, 10, 14.
    SEE ALSO Remote control
CHILI
    the comparative love of, 7
    craving, 27
CHIMPS, 45
CLAM CHOWDER, 17
CLUBS
    of cavemen, 81
    juggling, sexual performances with, 37
COFFEE, 28
    break, 64
    cold, bitter, 7
    SEE ALSO decaf
COMFY
    folding chairs, 56
    sofa, 75
COMIC BOOK, 18, 27
CONSPIRACY

THEORIES, 31
CORNFLAKES
    the desirability of sogginess in, 10
    Prozac in, 108
CORNSTARCH QUIP, 17
COUPON, 15
CREAM PUFF, 27

D

DART GAME, of love, 9
DEATH
    of clouds, 114
    disquisition on, 114
    of ducks, 114
    dying first, the consequences of, 100
    fight to the, 55
    freaked out by impending, 108
    the fun of, 81
    hamster section burial after, 100
    by humiliation, 21
    inevitability of, 20
    of trees, 114
DECAF, 10, 28.
    SEE ALSO coffee
DINOSAURS, 45, 118
    pop-up book, 54
DIP, 28
DOG MOVIE-STARS, 50
"D'OHH," 54
DOODADS, 38
DREAMS
    coffee break, 64
    death, 44
    odd, 31
    by slugs, 50
    sweet, 88
DROOL, 16
DUKE OF PRUNES, 107

E

EASTER BUNNY, lie of the, 117
ECOSYSTEM, 18
EMBALMER, 100
ENLIGHTENMENT, Binky's search for, 85
EROTO-HAMSTERS, 52

F

FAMILY VALUES, 39, 41, 42, 69
FASHION MODELS, 22
FDA, 26
FASHIONVILLE, 28
FETISH(ES)
    inflatable hat, 37
    objects, 37, 79, 96
    unspeakable, 19
FINGER FEELING, by Akbar & Jeff, 47, 52, 58, 61, 122
FIRST DATE CONVERSATIONAL NO-NOS, 31
FLABBOLEUM, 9
FLAG SALUTE, 107
FLU CHECKLIST, 82
FLY SWATTER, as sexual accoutrement, 96
FORKS, 30
FOUR MAGIC WORDS, 25
FRENCH FRIES, 11, 20
FUNWEAR, exploitative, 37, 68, 96

G

GHOST, 77
GIANT
    Bongo, 35
    eel, 75
    space caterpillar, 15
GNAT, attention span of, 95
GOD

gift to women by, 26
the lie about, 117
GOLFING
    ENTHUSIASTS, 56
GRAND WAZOO, 107
GRIPING READERS,
    a riposte to, 9
GRIZZLY BEAR, 27
GROENING
    Abe, 54, 76, 81, 83
    Will, 83, 91
        questions of, 76,
            88, 114
        stories by, 77, 81
        "why," 88
GRUNGE, 45
GUACAMOLE, 31
GUILLOTINE, 44
GUTS, lousy, the hatred
    of, 61

H

HAIRNET, 17
HARPOONIN', 55
HATE RAYS, 24
HATS
    baseball cap, 56
    beanie with
        propeller, 25
    beret, 56
    bone, 64
    with dangly balls, 24
    fez, find 'em yourself
        bonebrain
    hairnet, 17
    sailor, 36
    SEE ALSO Toupee
HEAD EXPLOSIONS,
    53, 65, 66
    ramifications of, 67
HEAD LICE, 45
HEXXON, 86
HIGH JINKS, sexual, the
    craving for, 10

HILLBILLY
    HOLLERING, 45
HOKEY POKEY, 26
HORNETS, inside your
    brain, 53, 70.
    SEE Yellow jackets
HOT RATS, 107
HUMAN FLESH, the
    gustatory properties
    of, 50

I

ICE CREAM, 13, 15, 119
    Häagen-Dazs, 22
IDLE PROMISES, 78
INFECTIOUS MEDICAL
    WASTE, 38
INFOMERCIALS, 26
INSCRUTABILITY, in
    revenge, 87
INSECTICIDE, the smell
    of, 26
        INSOMNIA, 19

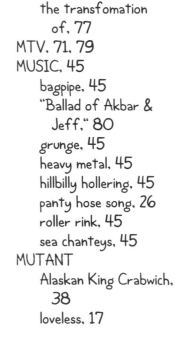

        IRAQ, the
        bombing
        of,
        98, 102

J

JAUNTY TUNE, the
    whistling of, 82
JENKINS FILE, 20
JUMBO TOWELETTES,
    38
JUMPER CABLES, 26

K

KETCHUP PACKETS, 11

L

LAVA, 45
LEDERHOSEN, 105
LETTERMAN, 10
LIMERICKS, 45
LINT, 28
LIONS
    bedtime stories, 77,
        88, 114
    classification of big
        cats, 83
"LOOK OF LOVE," 9
LOOSE THREAD, the
    triumph of, 97
LORD, 20
LOTTERY TICKETS,
    22, 75, 120
LOVE
    extortion of, 116
    at first sight, 8, 32
    replaced by food, 119
LOVE'S LITTLE
    KERNEL, 115
LUST-WEASELS, 52

M

MAGIC TRICKS, 7, 25, 26
MAMBO, 20, 28
MANSON FAMILY
    VALUES, 41
MANTRA, 75
MARRIAGE
    PROPOSALS, 18, 38
MARTIANS, in disguise, 50
METAL DETECTORS, 38
MEXICAN HAIRLESS,
    shivering of a,
    82
MIND READING,
    30
MR. BIG MOUTH,
    31
MOMMY, 8, 14
MOTHRA, 76

the transfomation
    of, 77
MTV, 71, 79
MUSIC, 45
    bagpipe, 45
    "Ballad of Akbar &
        Jeff," 80
    grunge, 45
    heavy metal, 45
    hillbilly hollering, 45
    panty hose song, 26
    roller rink, 45
    sea chanteys, 45
MUTANT
    Alaskan King Crabwich,
        38
    loveless, 17

N

NAKED FROLICKING, 63,
    72, 73, 78, 80, 116
    on book cover, 101
    in detention, 92
NAUGHTY PARTS, a-
    dangling from
        lederhosen, 105
NEW ZEALAND, sudden
    urge to move to, 12
NOSE NAMES
    blimp-, 9
    -boy, 16
    King Proboscis, 16
    loaf-of-bread-, 11
NUDE
    postcards, 38
    Republicans, 27

    O
OBJECT,
    blunt,
    uncontro-
    lable
    employment

of, 10
OCEAN FREIGHTER,
    sunken, 75
OINTMENT, 27
OTTERS, stubborn, 86
OVERBITE, 12.
    SEE EVERY PAGE

P

PANTY HOSE, 26, 37, 96
PARROTS
    SQUAWKING, 45
PASSION-DUCKS, 52
PEANUT BRITTLE, 101
PERSONAL ADS, 20
PERVO-GOATS, 52
PHLEGMMANIA, 82
PHONE ANWERING
    MACHINE, 9, 15, 20,
    45
PICASSO, Pablo, 15
PICTIONARY, 27
PIGSTY, 34
PILLOW
    ambivalent feelings
        for, 53
    talk, 9
"PIN THE TAIL ON
    YOUR INNER
        DONKEY," 9
PLAYGROUND SEESAW
    STRADDLING, 79
POLKA DOTS, 100
PRIMORDIAL OOZE
    NOISES, 45
PROZAC
    in action, 121
    for breakfast, 108
    theft of, 122
PTERODACTYL, 45, 54

Q

QUAYLE, Dan 16

I AM SEXUALLY AROUSED BY DAN QUAYLE. aroused sexually by, 43. SEE ALSO Sleazeball, right-wing

QUICKSAND, 70

QUIVERING
the allure of, 8
fool, 17
nervous wreck, 9

R

RADIATION EXPERIMENTS, 110
REMOTE CONTROL, 14, 70
request to run, 9
SEE Channel, the changing of
REPUBLICAN, 27, 43
nudist, 27
RICE CAKES, 31
ROBOTS, 50
ROOT CANAL SURGERY, 13
ROPE TRICKS, 39, 69, 89
RUBBER DOG TOYS, 30

S

SAFE-SEX CHARLIE, 26
SANTA CLAUS, the lie of, 117
SCAT SINGING, 103
SCORPION ALIEN HEAD, 91
SEA CHANTEYS, 45
SELF-MUTILATION, 71, 79
SEWER(S), 31
dog, 58
SEXIST PIG

place in history of, 111
self-recriminations of a, 16
SHARK WITHOUT A NAME, 88
SHOPPING, 15
SIMPSONS, 41
Bart, tattoo, 71
Bart, T-shirt, 68
"D'ohh," 54
hatred of, 62
Homer, 54
Marge, naked, 62
SINGLE WOMAN'S DIET, 22
SKULL, 118
SKULL BASHING
with blunt object, 10
hurt feelings due to, 61
with large rock, 22
during sleep, 109
therapeutic benefits of, 90
SLAMMER, 87
SLEAZEBALL, right-wing, 93.
SEE ALSO Bush; Quayle
SLUGS
dreams, 50
the rapture of sea, 7
SNOW GLOBES, 31
SOUL-MATE, coupling with so-called, 7
SPACESHIPS, 118
SPITE, 47
SPOONS, 30
SPOTTED OWL, 18
SQUIRREL(S)
frolicsome little smut-, 52
jabber, 45
squirrely girly, 9
STAR TREK, 26
STEGOSAURUS, 54

STRESS, 56
and complexion, 31
as giant eel, 75
as mantra, 75
"to the max," 75
as result of diet, 119
stressful intimacy, 31
STUNTS, 38
STYROFOAM, 20
packing pellets, 100
SUPER MARIO, 20

T

TAR
bits, 38
pits, 45
remover, 38
TARTAR SAUCE, 17, 38
TATTOO(S)
Hut, 71
secret, 31
TEN MAGIC WORDS, 26
THERAPIST
Mr. Big Mouth, 31
psychiatric diagnosis of, 80
punching out of, 27
vs. therapist, 90
THERAPY
armchair, 8
boring, painful, and expensive, 8
Couples Therapy Center, 109
in doodle form, 16
group session, 89
years on the couch, 108
THREE STOOGES BLOOPERS, 9
"THREE STRIKES YOU'RE OUT," 104
TINGLING, below the

waist, 12
TOBACCO CHEWING, 31
TOMB OF THE UNKNOWN BACHELOR, 20
TOMBSTONE, the spraying of polka dots on, 100
TOOTH FAIRY, lie of the, 117
TORTURE, 32
of hair, 24
X-mas, 113
TOUCH-MONKEYS, 52
TOUPEE, 44, 107
TOY(S)
boy, Abe the, 81
sex, inflatable, 37
TRAMPOLINE, 37
TRICKLE-DOWN ECONOMICS, 42
TRINKETS, 38

U

UNIVERSE, 31
cosmic union with, 108

V

VALENTINE'S GREETINGS, 11
VCR, the heaving of, 87
VIDEO
dating service, 21
game music, 45
games, 15, 20
VIDEOS
PLANET OF THE APES, 10
STAR TREK, 26
VOMIT, as cheer inducement, 59

W

WAFFLES, disgust with chewing of, 56
WALLOWING, 20

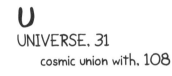

in trash, 9
in bitterness, 15
WALRUS, 83
WARTS, genital, 71
WHAAT?!!, 81
WHIMPERING, 14, 19
WILLIE HORTON, 42
WOOLLY MAMMOTHS, 45
breath, 111
WOUNDED INNER CHILD, 109

X

X-MAS PRESENT
offering self as, 57
the quandary of, 118
torture with, 113

Y

YEE-HAW, 33, 46
YELLOW JACKETS, 38
YELLOW SHARKS, 107
YUPPIE SCUM, 111

Z

ZAPPA, FRANK, 107
"ZIP-A-DEE-DOO-DAH," 53
ZOOKEEPER, 88